ACHIEVE LEVEL 5

MATHEMATICS

By Richard Cooper

RISING ★ STARS

PLEASE NOTE: THIS BOOK MAY NOT BE PHOTOCOPIED OR REPRODUCED AND WE APPRECIATE YOUR HELP IN PROTECTING OUR COPYRIGHT.

Rising Stars UK Ltd, 76 Farnaby Road, Bromley, BR1 4BH
www.risingstars-uk.com

Every effort has been made to trace copyright holders and obtain their permission for the use of copyright material. The authors and publishers will gladly receive information enabling them to rectify any error or omission in subsequent editions.

All facts are correct at time of going to press.

Published 2002
New Edition 2002
Reprinted 2002
New Edition 2003
Reprinted 2004 (twice), 2005
This full colour edition 2005
Text, design and layout © Rising Stars UK Ltd.

Educational consultants: Jon Kurta and Louise Moore
Design: Branford Graphics
Illustrations: Burville Riley, Beehive Illustration (Theresa Tibbetts) and Ken Vail Graphic Design
Cover image: Beehive Illustration (Theresa Tibbetts)
Cover design: Burville Riley

All rights reserved. No part of this publication may be reproduced, stored in a retrieval system, or transmitted, in any form by any means, electronic, mechanical, photocopying, recording or otherwise, without the prior permission of Rising Stars.

British Library Cataloguing in Publication Data
A CIP record for this book is available from the British Library.

ISBN 1-905056-06-0

Printed by Craft Print International Ltd, Singapore

Contents

How to use this book	4
Achieve Level 5 Maths – Objectives	6
Section 1: Level 4 – The Tricky Bits	8
Section 2: Level 5	
The Number System and Calculations	14
Measures, Shape and Space	30
Handling Data	46
Section 3: Using and Applying Mathematics	52
Key Facts	60
Tips and technique	62
Answers	63

How to use this book

What we have included:
★ Those topics at Level 4 that are trickiest to get right.
★ All Level 5 content so you know that you are covering all the topics that you need to understand in order to achieve a Level 5.

1 Introduction – This section tells you what you need to do to get to Level 5. It picks out the key learning objective and explains it simply to you.

2 Self assessment – Colour in the face that best describes your understanding of this concept.

3 Question – The question helps you to learn by doing. It is presented in a similar way to a SATs question and gives you a real example to work with.

4 Flow chart – This shows you the steps to use when completing questions like this. Some of the advice appears on every flow chart (read the question then read it again). This is because this is the best way of getting good marks in the test.

This icon indicates the section is a *teaching* section.

5 Tip boxes – These provide test hints and general tips on the topic.

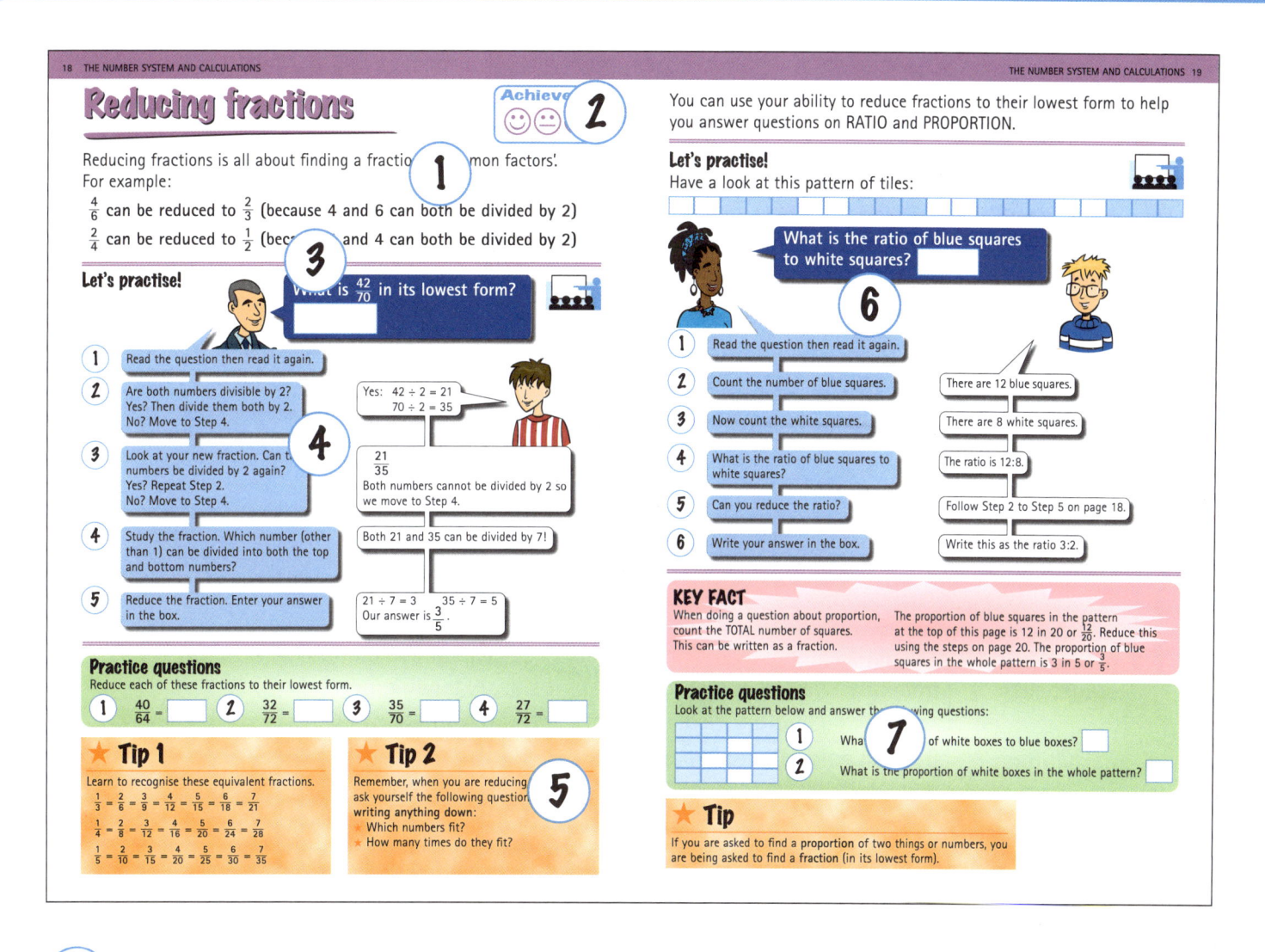

Reducing fractions

Reducing fractions is all about finding a fraction's 'common factors'. For example:

$\frac{4}{6}$ can be reduced to $\frac{2}{3}$ (because 4 and 6 can both be divided by 2)

$\frac{2}{4}$ can be reduced to $\frac{1}{2}$ (because 2 and 4 can both be divided by 2)

Let's practise!

What is $\frac{42}{70}$ in its lowest form?

1. Read the question then read it again.
2. Are both numbers divisible by 2? Yes? Then divide them both by 2. No? Move to Step 4.
   - Yes: 42 ÷ 2 = 21
   - 70 ÷ 2 = 35
3. Look at your new fraction. Can the numbers be divided by 2 again? Yes? Repeat Step 2. No? Move to Step 4.
   - $\frac{21}{35}$
   - Both numbers cannot be divided by 2 so we move to Step 4.
4. Study the fraction. Which number (other than 1) can be divided into both the top and bottom numbers?
   - Both 21 and 35 can be divided by 7!
5. Reduce the fraction. Enter your answer in the box.
   - 21 ÷ 7 = 3   35 ÷ 7 = 5
   - Our answer is $\frac{3}{5}$.

Practice questions
Reduce each of these fractions to their lowest form.

1. $\frac{40}{64} =$ ☐   2. $\frac{32}{72} =$ ☐   3. $\frac{35}{70} =$ ☐   4. $\frac{27}{72} =$ ☐

★ **Tip 1**
Learn to recognise these equivalent fractions.
$\frac{1}{3} = \frac{2}{6} = \frac{3}{9} = \frac{4}{12} = \frac{5}{15} = \frac{6}{18} = \frac{7}{21}$
$\frac{1}{4} = \frac{2}{8} = \frac{3}{12} = \frac{4}{16} = \frac{5}{20} = \frac{6}{24} = \frac{7}{28}$
$\frac{1}{5} = \frac{2}{10} = \frac{3}{15} = \frac{4}{20} = \frac{5}{25} = \frac{6}{30} = \frac{7}{35}$

★ **Tip 2**
Remember, when you are reducing, ask yourself the following questions before writing anything down:
★ Which numbers fit?
★ How many times do they fit?

You can use your ability to reduce fractions to their lowest form to help you answer questions on RATIO and PROPORTION.

Let's practise!
Have a look at this pattern of tiles:

What is the ratio of blue squares to white squares? ☐

1. Read the question then read it again.
2. Count the number of blue squares.
   - There are 12 blue squares.
3. Now count the white squares.
   - There are 8 white squares.
4. What is the ratio of blue squares to white squares?
   - The ratio is 12:8.
5. Can you reduce the ratio?
   - Follow Step 2 to Step 5 on page 18.
6. Write your answer in the box.
   - Write this as the ratio 3:2.

KEY FACT
When doing a question about proportion, count the TOTAL number of squares. This can be written as a fraction.

The proportion of blue squares in the pattern at the top of this page is 12 in 20 or $\frac{12}{20}$. Reduce this using the steps on page 20. The proportion of blue squares in the whole pattern is 3 in 5 or $\frac{3}{5}$.

Practice questions
Look at the pattern below and answer the following questions:

1. What is the ratio of white boxes to blue boxes? ☐
2. What is the proportion of white boxes in the whole pattern? ☐

★ **Tip**
If you are asked to find a **proportion** of two things or numbers, you are being asked to find a **fraction** (in its lowest form).

---

6 Second question – On most pages there will be a second question. This will either look at a slightly different question type or give you another example to work through.

7 Practice questions – This is where you have to do the work! Try each question using the technique in the flow chart then check your answers at the back. Practising questions is the best way to help improve your understanding.

GOOD LUCK!

Achieve Level 5 Maths – Objectives

This chart allows you to see which objectives in the National Numeracy Strategy have been covered and which are to be completed.

We have matched the objectives directly with each page of Achieve Level 5 so you can monitor progress.

When children have indicated 'achievement', you can encourage them to tick the box or highlight that row in this table. That way, you and your class know what has been achieved and what is still to be covered.

Text in **bold** denotes key objectives.

Page no.	Title	Objective	Achieved? (tick)
Level 4 – the Tricky Bits			
8	Predicting sequences	Recognise and extend number sequences formed by counting from any number in steps of constant size, extending beyond zero when counting back (Numbers and the Number System)	
9	Calculators	Develop calculator skills and use a calculator effectively (Calculations)	
10	Perimeter	Measure and calculate the perimeter of rectangles and other simple shapes, using counting methods and standard units (Measures)	
11	The 24 hour clock	Use units of time; read the time on a 24 hour digital clock and use 24 hour clock notation, such as 19:53 (Measures)	
12	Reading scales	Record estimates and readings from scales to a suitable degree of accuracy (Measures)	
13	Venn diagrams	Solve a problem by collecting quickly, organising, representing and interpreting data in Venn diagrams (Handling Data)	
The Number System and Calculations			
14–15	Checking your answers	Check with the inverse operation Estimate by approximating (round to the nearest 10 or a 100), then check result	
16–17	Decimals	**Extend written methods to short multiplication/division of numbers involving decimals** **Extend written methods to column addition and subtraction of numbers involving decimals** Use brackets	
18–19	Reducing fractions	**Reduce a fraction to its simplest form by cancelling common factors** in the numerator and denominator Solve simple problems involving ratio and proportion	
20–21	Calculating fractions or percentages	**Use a fraction as an 'operator' to find fractions**, including tenths and hundredths, **of numbers or quantities** Develop calculator skills and use a calculator effectively **Find simple percentages of small whole-number quantities**	

22–23	Multiplication and division	Extend written methods to long multiplication of a 3-digit by a 2-digit integer; division of HTU by TU Derive quickly: division facts corresponding to tables up to 10 × 10 Approximate first. Use informal pencil and paper methods to support record or explain multiplications or divisions	
24–25	Negative numbers	Find the difference between a positive and negative integer, or two negative integers, in a context such as temperature or the number line, and order a set of negative integers	
26–27	Simple formulae	Develop from explaining a generalised relationship in words to expressing it in a formula using letters as symbols	
28–29	Using brackets	Understand and use the relationships between the four operations and the principles (not the names) of the arithmetic laws Use brackets	
Measures, Shape and Space			
30–32	Coordinates	Read and plot coordinates in all four quadrants	
33–37	Angles	Use a protractor to measure and draw angles to the nearest degree Calculate angles in a triangle or around a point	
38–41	Symmetries of 2D shapes	Recognise where a shape will be after reflection: in a mirror line touching the shape at a point; in two mirror lines at right angles Recognise where a shape will be after two translations	
42–43	Units of measure	Use, read and write standard metric units (km, m, cm, mm, kg, g, l, ml, cl), including their abbreviations, and relationships between them Convert smaller to larger units and vice versa Identify and use appropriate operations (including combinations of operations) to solve word problems involving numbers and quantities based on 'real life', money or measures Know rough equivalents of lb kg, oz and g, miles and km, litres and pints or gallons	
44–45	The area of a rectangle	Understand area measured in square centimetres (cm^2) Understand and use the formula in words 'length × breadth' for the area of a rectangle Calculate the area of simple compound shapes that can be split into rectangles	
Handling Data			
46	Finding the mean and median	Begin to find the median and mean of a set of data	
47	Finding the range and mode	Find the mode and range of a set of data	
48–49	Graphs and pie charts	Solve a problem by representing, extracting and interpreting data in graphs, charts and diagrams, including those generated by computer, for example: line graphs for distance/time and conversions	
50–51	The probability scale	Use the language associated with probability to discuss events, including those with equally likely outcomes	
Using and Applying Mathematics			
52–59	Using and applying mathematics – solving problems	Choose and use appropriate number operations to solve problems and appropriate ways of calculating: mental, mental with jottings, written methods, calculator. Explain methods and reasoning, orally and in writing Solve mathematical problems or puzzles, recognise and explain patterns and relationships, generalise and predict Identify and use appropriate operations (including combinations of operations) to solve word problems involving numbers and quantities based on 'real life', money or measures, using one or more steps. Explain methods and reasoning	

Predicting sequences

Achieved?

This is not as difficult as it sounds. Sequences and patterns just can't live without each other!

Just remember: sequence = numbers following a pattern.

Pattern 1
The pattern may mean the difference between numbers is always the same:
  2   4   6   8   10
    +2   +2   +2   +2

Pattern 2
The pattern may mean the difference between numbers changes according to a rule:
  5   11   23   41   65
    +6   +12   +18   +24

Let's practise!

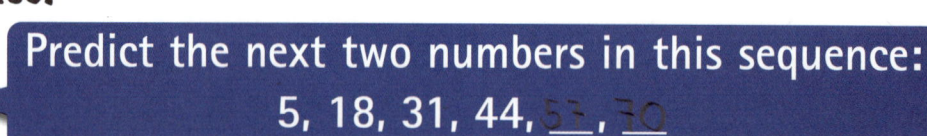

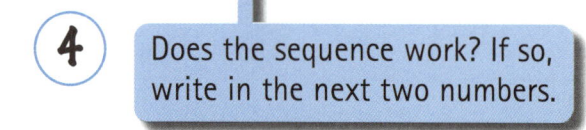

Predict the next two numbers in this sequence:
5, 18, 31, 44, 57, 70

(1) Read the question then read it again.

(2) Study the numbers.

What is the pattern?

What is the difference between the numbers?
5 + ? = 18   ? = 13
18 + ? = 31   ? = 13

(3) Test the pattern.

Is the difference between all the numbers 13?
  5   18   31   44   57   70
    +13   +13   +13   +13   +13

(4) Does the sequence work? If so, write in the next two numbers.

Yes, the pattern works and the next numbers in the sequence are 57 and 70.

Practice questions
Find the missing numbers in these sequences.

(1) 29, 35, 41, 47, 53, 59

(2) 114, 131, __, __, 182, __

(3) 19, 8, −3, −14, __, __

★ Tip 1
You will see the pattern more easily if you write in the numbers underneath the sequence.
  4   14   34   64
    +10   +20   +30

★ Tip 2
A sequence may be shown in pictures. Just turn the pictures into numbers to help you see the pattern.
★   ★★   ★★   ★★★★
           ★★   ★★★

It can be written as:
  1   2   4   7
    +1   +2   +3

Calculators

Achieved? 😊 😐 ☹

Calculators can be seen as the answer to everything in Maths. If used correctly they are a useful tool, but when used incorrectly they can become a nightmare!

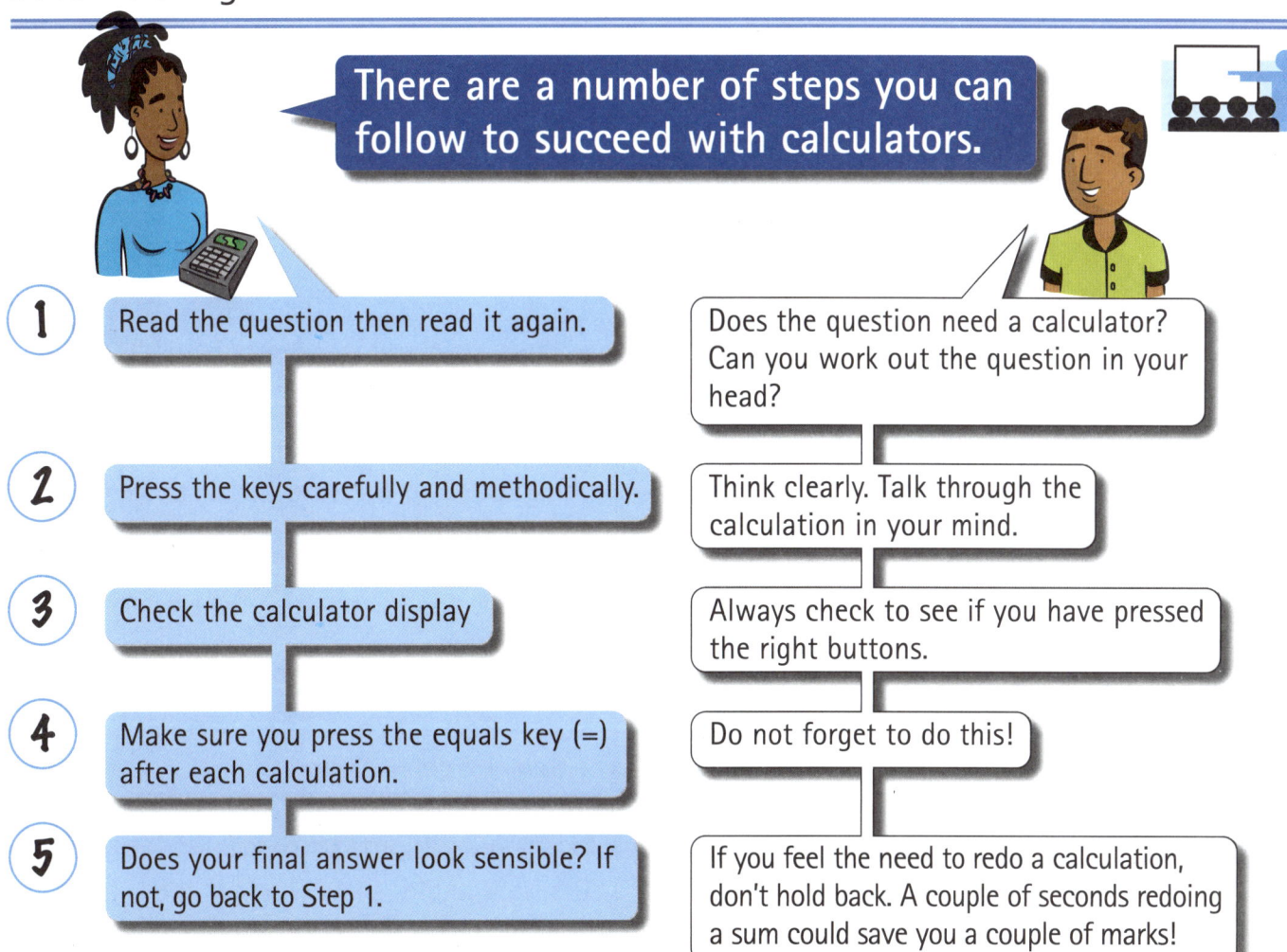

There are a number of steps you can follow to succeed with calculators.

1. Read the question then read it again. — Does the question need a calculator? Can you work out the question in your head?

2. Press the keys carefully and methodically. — Think clearly. Talk through the calculation in your mind.

3. Check the calculator display — Always check to see if you have pressed the right buttons.

4. Make sure you press the equals key (=) after each calculation. — Do not forget to do this!

5. Does your final answer look sensible? If not, go back to Step 1. — If you feel the need to redo a calculation, don't hold back. A couple of seconds redoing a sum could save you a couple of marks!

Practice questions
Try these sums on your calculator.

1. 849 + 528 =
2. 606 − 6.6 =
3. 894 ÷ 24 =
4. 43 × 7.6 =
5. 883 × 8.83 =
6. 202 ÷ 0.02 =

★ **Tip 1**
Don't forget to press the decimal point key when keying in decimal numbers.
3.5 = [3] [.] [5]

★ **Tip 2**
As you press each button, check to see what appears on the display.

Perimeter

Achieved?

Let's look at how to calculate the perimeter of a shape.

A common mistake is to forget one side of a shape when measuring it!

KEY FACT
The perimeter is the total distance around the outside of a shape.

Let's practise!

What is the perimeter of this shape?

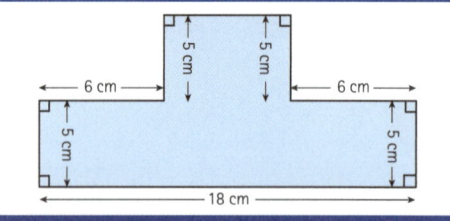

(shape with measurements: 5 cm, 5 cm, 6 cm, 6 cm, 5 cm, 5 cm, 18 cm)

1 Read the question then read it again.
→ What are we being asked to do? We are being asked to measure the distance around the shape.

2 Choose a side to start from. Put a line through it with your pencil.
→ This helps you to remember where you started from.

3 Add up all the lengths that are given in the question. Mark them off as you go.
→ 5 cm + 6 cm + 5 cm + 18 cm + 5 cm + 6 cm + 5 cm = 23 cm

4 Now work out the lengths of the sides you haven't been given.
→ This is the IMPORTANT PART! The right angles show you that the distance along the top of the shape must be the same as the distance along the bottom. Both must be **18 cm**.

The **missing** side must be 6 cm because 6 cm + **6 cm** + 6 cm = **18 cm.**

5 Add the missing length to the total of the lengths you have been given (see Step 3).
→ 50 cm + 6 cm = 56 cm

6 Is your answer a sensible one? If so, put it in the box.
→ The perimeter of the shape is 56 cm.

★ Tip 1
Think of a perimeter fence going all the way round a football pitch.

★ Tip 2
Don't try to measure 'missing' sides with a ruler. The reason they are missing is because the test wants to see if you can work it out from the given lengths.

LEVEL 4 – THE TRICKY BITS 11

The 24 hour clock

Achieved?

You should be pretty good at telling the time by now, but certain questions can still cause problems. It is very easy to make silly mistakes when dealing with the 24 hour clock. When you are working out time it is important to take things step-by-step.

18.23

Let's practise!

How long is it from 03:14 to 21:26?

1. Read the question then read it again.
2. Picture the question. — Imagine the times. 03:14 is very early in the morning; 21:26 is late evening. The answer will be quite high.
3. Count the minutes round to the first hour. — 03:14 to 04:00 is 46 minutes.
4. Now count the hours round to the given hour. — 04:00 around to 21:00 is 17 hours.
5. Add up the minutes and convert to hours if you need to. — 46 minutes + the 26 minutes (from the time 21:26) is 72 minutes. 72 minutes = 1 hour and 12 minutes.
6. Calculate all the hours and add the remaining minutes to give a final answer. — 17 hours + 1 hour + 12 minutes = 18 hours and 12 minutes.
7. Does the answer look sensible? If so, put it in the box. — Yes, our answer looks sensible. 18 hours and 12 minutes is correct.

Practice questions
Work out the following times in hours and minutes.

1. 08:32 to 16:50
2. 10:54 to 19:21
3. 22:22 to 01:11
4. 18:59 to 23:03

★ **Tip 1**
Get used to reading timetables for buses, trains and aeroplanes. Test yourself on imaginary journeys.

★ **Tip 2**
Remember, when comparing times the **fastest** one is the **shortest** one.

Reading scales

Achieved?

We use scales to measure things. They are just like number lines! The tricky bit is remembering that you need to work out what each mark on the scale stands for.

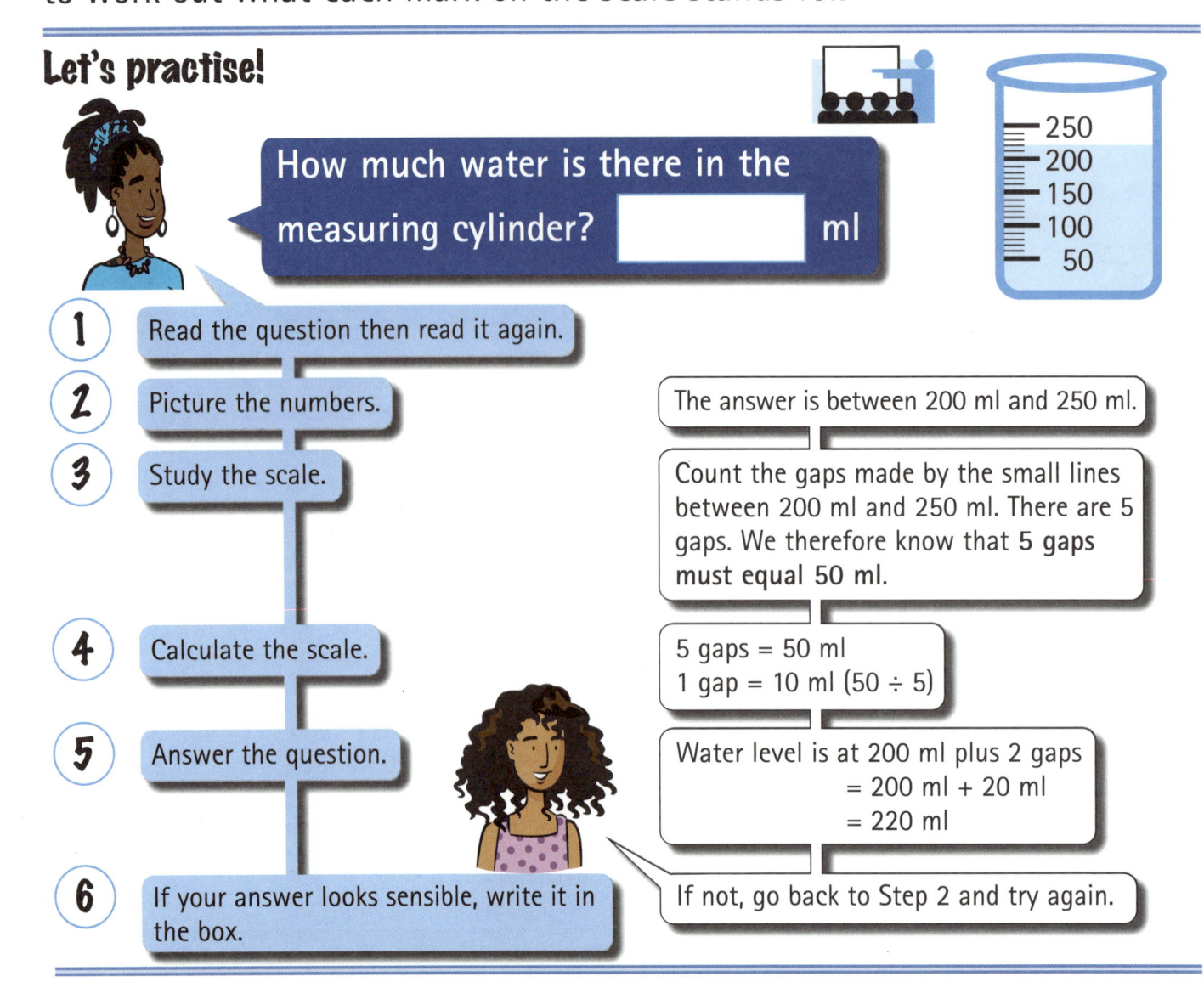

Let's practise!

How much water is there in the measuring cylinder? ☐ ml

1. Read the question then read it again.
2. Picture the numbers.
3. Study the scale.
4. Calculate the scale.
5. Answer the question.
6. If your answer looks sensible, write it in the box.

The answer is between 200 ml and 250 ml.

Count the gaps made by the small lines between 200 ml and 250 ml. There are 5 gaps. We therefore know that **5 gaps must equal 50 ml.**

5 gaps = 50 ml
1 gap = 10 ml (50 ÷ 5)

Water level is at 200 ml plus 2 gaps
= 200 ml + 20 ml
= 220 ml

If not, go back to Step 2 and try again.

Practice questions

How much water is in these measuring cylinders?

1. 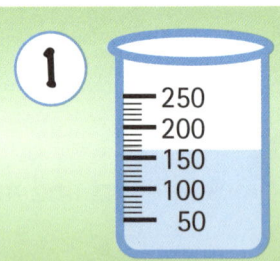 ☐
2.  ☐

★ Tip 1

Read scales very carefully and count the gaps more than once to be sure you have got it right. Write in missing measurements in pencil to help you remember them.

★ Tip 2

Always check your answer carefully to be sure it makes sense.

Venn diagrams

Venn diagrams may sound complicated but really they are just a way of sorting information into groups. Look at the diagram. There are three regions – A, B and C.

Region A belongs to group A.
Region B belongs to group B.
Region C belongs to group A and group B.

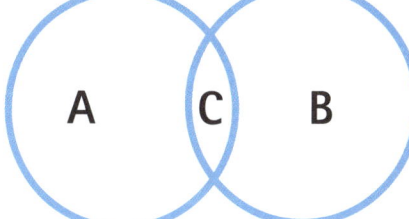

Let's practise!

Look at this table and sort the names into the Venn diagram. Decide on a description for each region.

Name	Likes swimming	Likes cycling
Ellie	✗	✓
Ryan	✓	✗
Junior	✓	✓
Abarna	✗	✓
Nirogini	✓	✗
Lisa	✓	✓
Alex	✗	✓

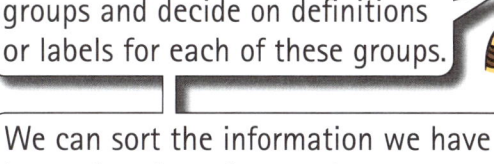

1. Read the question then read it again.

   We need to sort the names into groups and decide on definitions or labels for each of these groups.

2. Study the information given.

   We can sort the information we have been given into three main groups: Group A (children who like swimming), Group B (children who like cycling) and Group C (children who like swimming **and** cycling).

3. Sort the information.

   Write out the groups on rough paper first.

4. Check your answer against your table.

   Check back to make sure you have included all the children in the right groups before completing your answer.

THE NUMBER SYSTEM AND CALCULATIONS

Checking your answers

Achieved?

Inverse operations

Remember, adding and subtracting are OPPOSITES. Multiplying and dividing are OPPOSITES. We can use this knowledge to check our calculations quickly.

e.g.   75 + 85 = 160   CHECK   160 − 85 = 75
or   42 × 6 = 252   CHECK   252 ÷ 6 = 42
INVERSE means the same as OPPOSITE

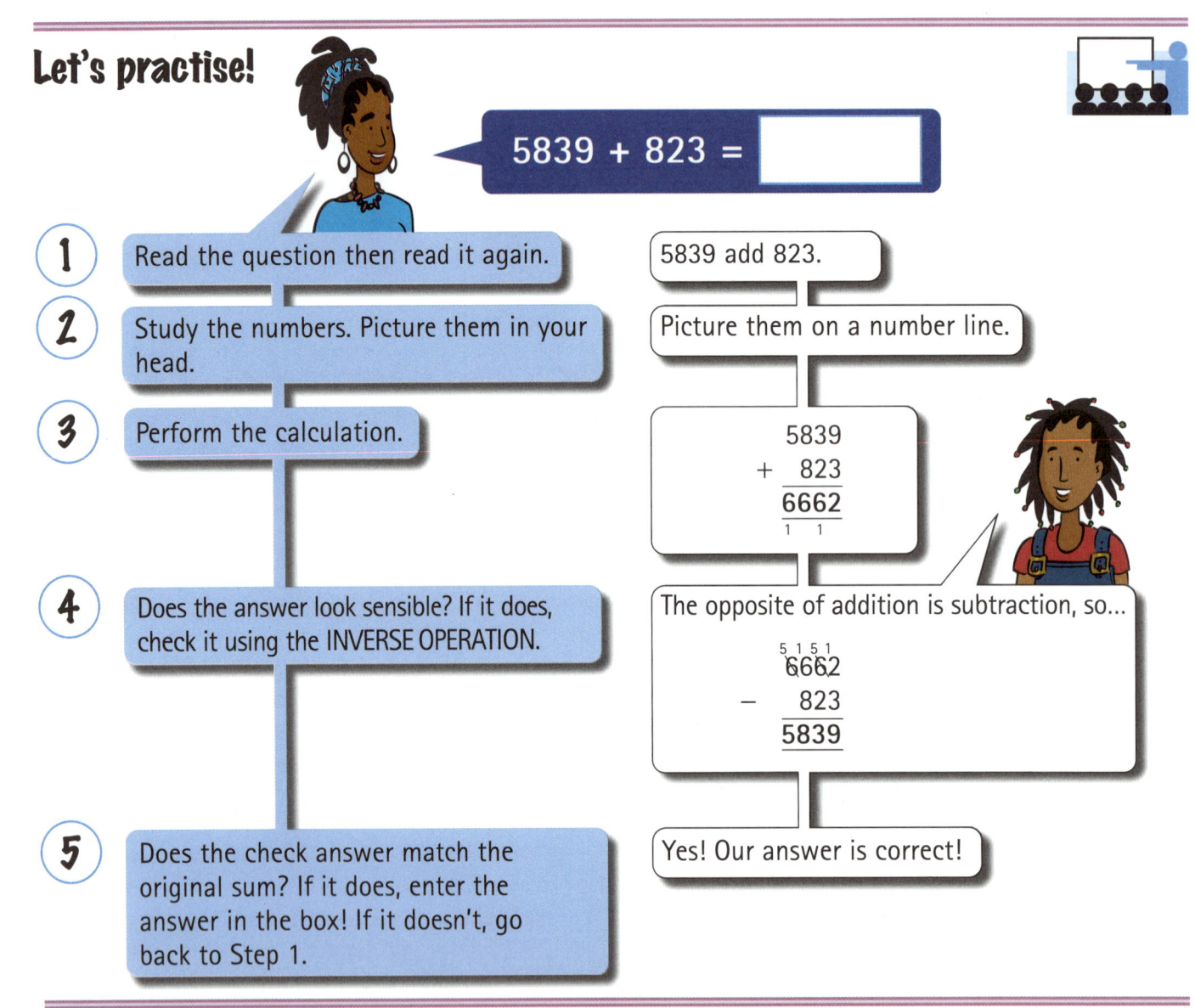

Let's practise!

5839 + 823 = ☐

1. Read the question then read it again.
   — 5839 add 823.

2. Study the numbers. Picture them in your head.
   — Picture them on a number line.

3. Perform the calculation.

   ```
     5839
   +  823
   ─────
     6662
     1 1
   ```

4. Does the answer look sensible? If it does, check it using the INVERSE OPERATION.
   — The opposite of addition is subtraction, so…

   ```
     5 1 5 1
     6 6 6 2
   −    823
   ─────
     5839
   ```

5. Does the check answer match the original sum? If it does, enter the answer in the box! If it doesn't, go back to Step 1.
   — Yes! Our answer is correct!

Practice questions

Do these calculations and then check your answers using the inverse operation.

1. 74 × 45 = ☐
2. 792 + 445 = ☐
3. 24 624 ÷ 36 = ☐
4. 5823 − 771 = ☐

★ **Tip**

Get into the habit of checking your answers. It may help you do better in your test!

THE NUMBER SYSTEM AND CALCULATIONS 15

Rounding up or down

Another excellent way to check your answers is to round the numbers in the question up or down. Doing this will give you a simple sum to do and give you a rough answer.

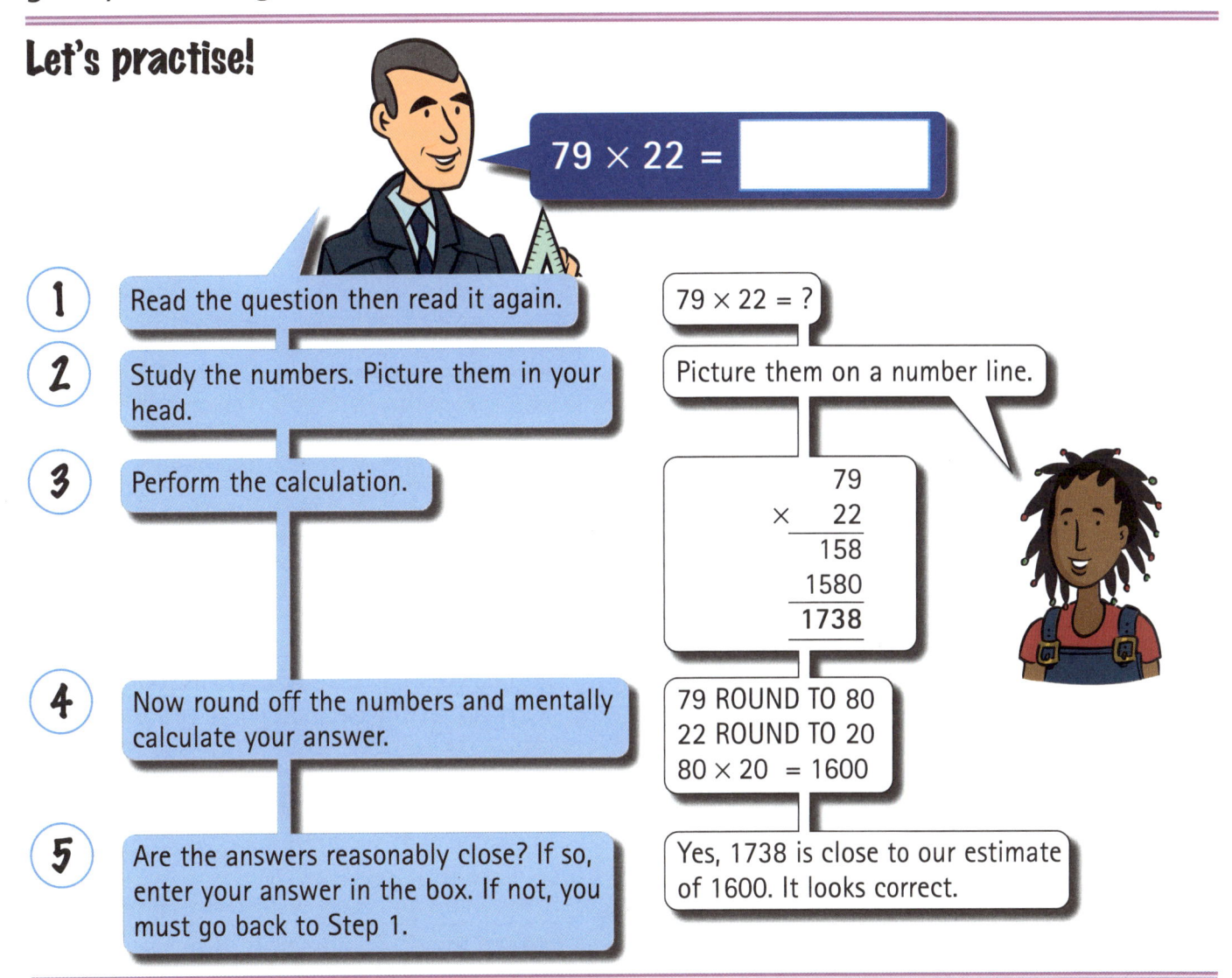

Let's practise!

79 × 22 =

1. Read the question then read it again.
2. Study the numbers. Picture them in your head.
3. Perform the calculation.
4. Now round off the numbers and mentally calculate your answer.
5. Are the answers reasonably close? If so, enter your answer in the box. If not, you must go back to Step 1.

79 × 22 = ?

Picture them on a number line.

$$\begin{array}{r} 79 \\ \times\ 22 \\ \hline 158 \\ 1580 \\ \hline 1738 \end{array}$$

79 ROUND TO 80
22 ROUND TO 20
80 × 20 = 1600

Yes, 1738 is close to our estimate of 1600. It looks correct.

Practice questions
Do these calculations and then check your answers using the 'Rounding up or down' technique.

1. 31 × 59 =
2. 7992 − 295 =
3. 8192 + 209 =
4. 882 ÷ 18 =

★ Tip 1
When rounding up or down think of 'friendly' numbers. These are numbers you can work with easily in your head. Some examples are 2, 5, 10, 50, 100 and so on.

★ Tip 2
Get used to doing mental calculations every day. Give your brain 'gym exercises' to do which involve calculating numbers quickly. Darts can be a fun way to do this!

16   THE NUMBER SYSTEM AND CALCULATIONS

Decimals

Achieved?

To achieve Level 5 you must be able to work with numbers to two decimal places. Decimals are easy – remember, money is written with decimals! For example, £9.85 is nearly £10.00; 3.07 is a bit more than 3.

Let's practise!

Write in the missing number.
(5.22 − 3.79) + 4.8 = ?

1. Read the question then read it again.

   (5.22 − 3.79) + 4.8 =?

2. Picture the numbers. What do they look like?

   5.22 is close to 5… 3.79 is nearer to 4… 4.8 is close to 5…

3. Study the numbers again and think about them!

   5 − 4 = 1… 1 + 5 = 6.
   Look for the brackets. Remember, always do the bits in brackets first!

4. When adding and subtracting decimals, remove the decimal point and calculate.

   Set out your calculation like this. Don't worry about the decimal point yet.
   522 − 379 = 143
   143 + 480 = 623

5. Check back to your estimate at Step 3.

   You know that your number is going to be close to 6 (see Step 3).

6. Replace the decimal point.

   Replace the decimal point to match your estimate. Your answer is 6.23.

7. If your answer looks sensible, write it in the box.

   Check against your estimate, if it doesn't look right, go back to Step 3 and try again.

⭐ **Tip 1**

When rounding, remember 5 is always UP!

1.265 = 1.27

⭐ **Tip 2**

When writing money remember:
£0.45p (✗)   £0.45 (✓)
0.45p (✗)   45p (✓)
Say the answer to yourself before you write it down!

THE NUMBER SYSTEM AND CALCULATIONS   17

Let's practise!

Write in the missing number.

4.45 × 6.8 = ☐

1. Read the question then read it again.

4.45 × 6.8 = ?

2. Picture the numbers. What do they look like?

It's nearly 4 × 7.

3. Study the numbers again and think about them.

The answer will be more than 24 (4 × 6) and less than 35 (5 × 7).

4. Remember the rules!

Set out your calculation using the grid method. Don't worry about the decimal point yet.

×	400	40	5
60	24 000	2400	300
8	3200	320	40

= 26 700
= + 3 560
   30 260

5. Calculate.

Now put in the decimal point. Count three from the right. Your answer is 30.260 or 30.26!

6. Check your answer.

So, 4.45 × 6.8 = 30.26
30.26 is just over 30.

7. If your answer looks sensible, write it in the box. If not, go back to Step 3.

From Step 3 we know our answer should be between 24 and 35. Great!

Practice questions

Here are some questions for you to try.
Remember to use the step-by-step approach above. Write your answers to two decimal places.

1. 6.25 × 3.8 = ☐

2. (8.23 − 5.86) + 5.2 = ☐

3. (9.4 × 3.7) + 7.75 = ☐

4. £38 − (£4.53 ÷ 3) = ☐

THE NUMBER SYSTEM AND CALCULATIONS

Reducing fractions

Achieved?

Reducing fractions is all about finding a fraction's 'common factors'. For example:

$\frac{4}{6}$ can be reduced to $\frac{2}{3}$ (because 4 and 6 can both be divided by 2)

$\frac{2}{4}$ can be reduced to $\frac{1}{2}$ (because 2 and 4 can both be divided by 2)

Let's practise!

What is $\frac{42}{70}$ in its lowest form?

1. Read the question then read it again.

2. Are both numbers divisible by 2? Yes? Then divide them both by 2. No? Move to Step 4.

   Yes: $42 \div 2 = 21$
   $70 \div 2 = 35$

3. Look at your new fraction. Can the numbers be divided by 2 again? Yes? Repeat Step 2. No? Move to Step 4.

   $\frac{21}{35}$
   Both numbers cannot be divided by 2 so we move to Step 4.

4. Study the fraction. Which number (other than 1) can be divided into both the top and bottom numbers?

   Both 21 and 35 can be divided by 7!

5. Reduce the fraction. Enter your answer in the box.

   $21 \div 7 = 3$ $35 \div 7 = 5$
   Our answer is $\frac{3}{5}$.

Practice questions

Reduce each of these fractions to their lowest form.

1) $\frac{40}{64} =$ ☐   2) $\frac{32}{72} =$ ☐   3) $\frac{35}{70} =$ ☐   4) $\frac{27}{72} =$ ☐

★ Tip 1

Learn to recognise these equivalent fractions.

$\frac{1}{3} = \frac{2}{6} = \frac{3}{9} = \frac{4}{12} = \frac{5}{15} = \frac{6}{18} = \frac{7}{21}$

$\frac{1}{4} = \frac{2}{8} = \frac{3}{12} = \frac{4}{16} = \frac{5}{20} = \frac{6}{24} = \frac{7}{28}$

$\frac{1}{5} = \frac{2}{10} = \frac{3}{15} = \frac{4}{20} = \frac{5}{25} = \frac{6}{30} = \frac{7}{35}$

★ Tip 2

Remember, when you are reducing a fraction ask yourself the following questions **before** writing anything down:
★ Which numbers fit?
★ How many times do they fit?

THE NUMBER SYSTEM AND CALCULATIONS 19

You can use your ability to reduce fractions to their lowest form to help you answer questions on RATIO and PROPORTION.

Let's practise!
Have a look at this pattern of tiles:

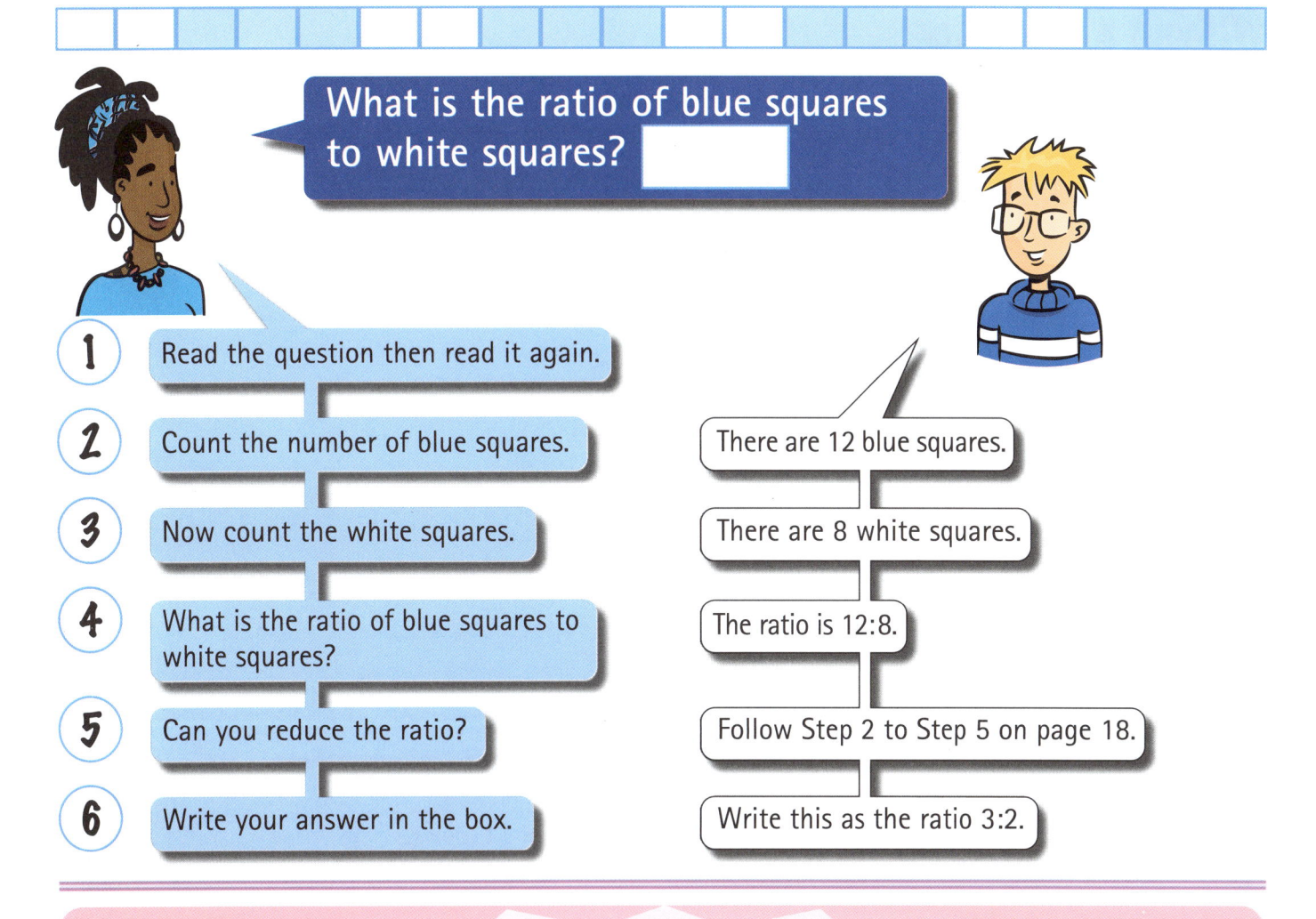

What is the ratio of blue squares to white squares?

1. Read the question then read it again.
2. Count the number of blue squares. — There are 12 blue squares.
3. Now count the white squares. — There are 8 white squares.
4. What is the ratio of blue squares to white squares? — The ratio is 12:8.
5. Can you reduce the ratio? — Follow Step 2 to Step 5 on page 18.
6. Write your answer in the box. — Write this as the ratio 3:2.

KEY FACT
When doing a question about proportion, count the TOTAL number of squares. This can be written as a fraction.

The proportion of blue squares in the pattern at the top of this page is 12 in 20 or $\frac{12}{20}$. Reduce this using the steps on page 20. The proportion of blue squares in the whole pattern is 3 in 5 or $\frac{3}{5}$.

Practice questions
Look at the pattern below and answer the following questions:

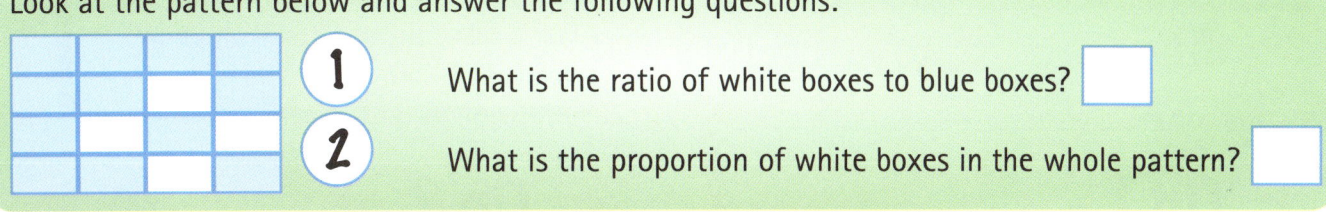

1. What is the ratio of white boxes to blue boxes?
2. What is the proportion of white boxes in the whole pattern?

★ Tip
If you are asked to find a **proportion** of two things or numbers, you are being asked to find a **fraction** (in its lowest form).

THE NUMBER SYSTEM AND CALCULATIONS

Calculating fractions or percentages

Achieved?

Without a calculator

Lots of questions that ask you to find fractions or percentages of things are easy to answer WITHOUT a calculator by just using some simple maths, such as doubling, halving or dividing by 10. For example:

70% of 900 metres

10% of 900 is 90

so 70% of 900 is 7 × 90

7 × 90 = 630

= 630 metres

Let's practise!

A new mobile phone costs £170. In the sales the price is reduced by 15%. What is the new price of the mobile?

1 Read the question then read it again. What am I being asked to do?

Find the NEW price of the mobile.

2 To find the discount, first calculate 10% of the original price.

10% of £170 = £17.

3 Now calculate 5% of the original price and add your answers together to find 15%.

5% is half of 10% so 5% is £8.50
(5%) + (10%) = (15%)
£8.50 + £17.00 = £25.50

4 Don't forget the next part! What is the NEW price of the mobile?

The mobile has been reduced by £25.50. So the new price is £170 − £25.50 = £144.50.

5 Check you have answered the question properly.

What is the new price of the mobile? After a discount of £25.50 the new price is £144.50.

★ Tip 1

To find 1% of something, first find 10% then find 10% of THAT answer. You can work out any % by adding all the 10%, 5% and 1% answers together!

★ Tip 2

Remember as many percentage/fraction equivalents as you can:

50% = $\frac{1}{2}$ 25% = $\frac{1}{4}$ 75% = $\frac{3}{4}$

33% = nearly $\frac{1}{3}$ 66% = nearly $\frac{2}{3}$

With a calculator

You can work out many fractions or percentages very easily without a calculator, but sometimes it's not so easy. For example, if you scored 15 out of 30 in your spelling test you should be able to recognise that you got 50% correct. If you improved the following week and got 24 out of 30 then you may need to use your calculator! Calculate as follows:

Key in [24] then [÷] then [30] then [%]

You should have the answer 80, which means you scored 80% correct.

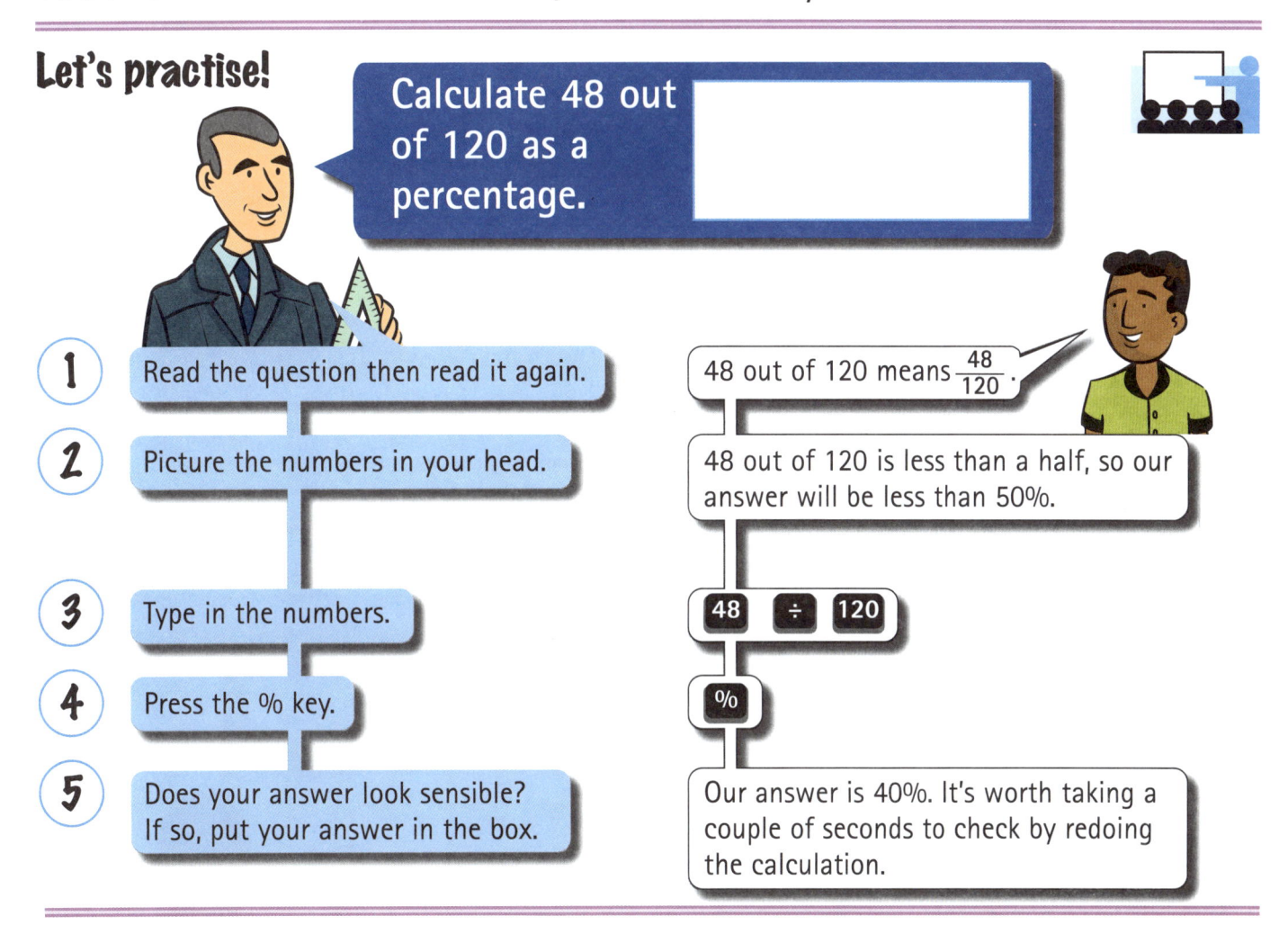

Let's practise!

Calculate 48 out of 120 as a percentage.

1. Read the question then read it again.
2. Picture the numbers in your head.
3. Type in the numbers.
4. Press the % key.
5. Does your answer look sensible? If so, put your answer in the box.

48 out of 120 means $\frac{48}{120}$.

48 out of 120 is less than a half, so our answer will be less than 50%.

[48] [÷] [120]

[%]

Our answer is 40%. It's worth taking a couple of seconds to check by redoing the calculation.

Practice questions
Work these out **without** a calculator.

1. 75% of 800 cm
2. 65% of 180 kg
3. 45% of £320
4. 15% of 220 km
5. 40% of 150 ml
6. 35% of £560

Practice questions
Answer these with a calculator (express them as a %).

1. $\frac{95}{250}$ =
2. $\frac{54}{360}$ =
3. $\frac{147}{420}$ =
4. $\frac{143}{220}$ =

Multiplication and division

Achieved? 😊 😐 ☹

To get a Level 5 you need to be able to multiply and divide a 3-digit number by a 2-digit number without a calculator. EASY!

Let's practise!

Write in the missing number. $489 \times 52 = \square$

1. Read the question then read it again.

   $489 \times 52 =$

2. Picture the numbers.

   489 rounds up to 500 and 52 rounds down to 50...

3. Study the numbers and think about them.

   489×52 is roughly $500 \times 50 =$ which is 25 000

4. Calculate your answer.

×	400	80	9	
50	20 000	4000	450	= 24 450
2	800	160	18	= + 978

   25 428

5. Does your answer look sensible? If it does then write it in the box. If it doesn't then go back to Step 3.

   25 428 is close to my estimate. The answer looks correct!

Write in the missing number. $212 \times 87 = \square$

1. Read the question then read it again.

   $212 \times 87 =$

2. Picture the numbers.

   212 is near 200 and 87 rounds to 90.

3. Study the numbers and think about them.

   212×87 is approximately $200 \times 90 = 18\,000$

4. Calculate your answer.

×	200	10	2	
80	16 000	800	160	= 16 960
7	1400	70	14	= + 1484

   18 444

5. Does your answer look sensible? If it does, write it in the box. If it doesn't, go back to Step 3.

   18 444 is very close to our estimate. It's a sensible answer!

THE NUMBER SYSTEM AND CALCULATIONS 23

Now let's try division!

Write in the missing number. 912 ÷ 19 = ☐

1. Read the question then read it again.

912 ÷ 19 =

2. Picture the numbers – what do they look like?

912 is close to 900 and 19 rounds up to 20.

3. Study the numbers and think about them.

912 ÷ 19 is approximately 900 ÷ 20 = 45

4. Calculate your answer.

912 − 760 (40 × 19) leaves 152
152 − 95 (5 × 19) leaves 57
57 − 57 (3 × 19) leaves 0
So 40 + 5 + 3 = 48

5. If your answer looks sensible, write it in the box.

Our answer of 48 is very close to our estimate of 45. Yes, it looks right.

KEY FACT × and ÷ are opposites

Use this fact to help with tricky questions. For example:

21 × 16 = 336   336 ÷ 21 = 16
16 × ☐ = 336   so   336 ÷ 16 = 21   Our missing number is 21.

Practice questions
Try these for practice.

1. 482 × 36 =
2. 993 × 75 =
3. 547 × 58 =
4. 728 × 23 =
5. 264 × 45 =

6. 812 ÷ 14 =
7. 621 ÷ 23 =
8. 924 ÷ 12 =
9. 935 ÷ 17 =
10. 486 ÷ 18 =

Negative numbers

Achieved?

Be positive! NEGATIVE NUMBERS ARE EASY. Imagine a thermometer and you have a number line with positive and negative numbers. So chill out and try this question.

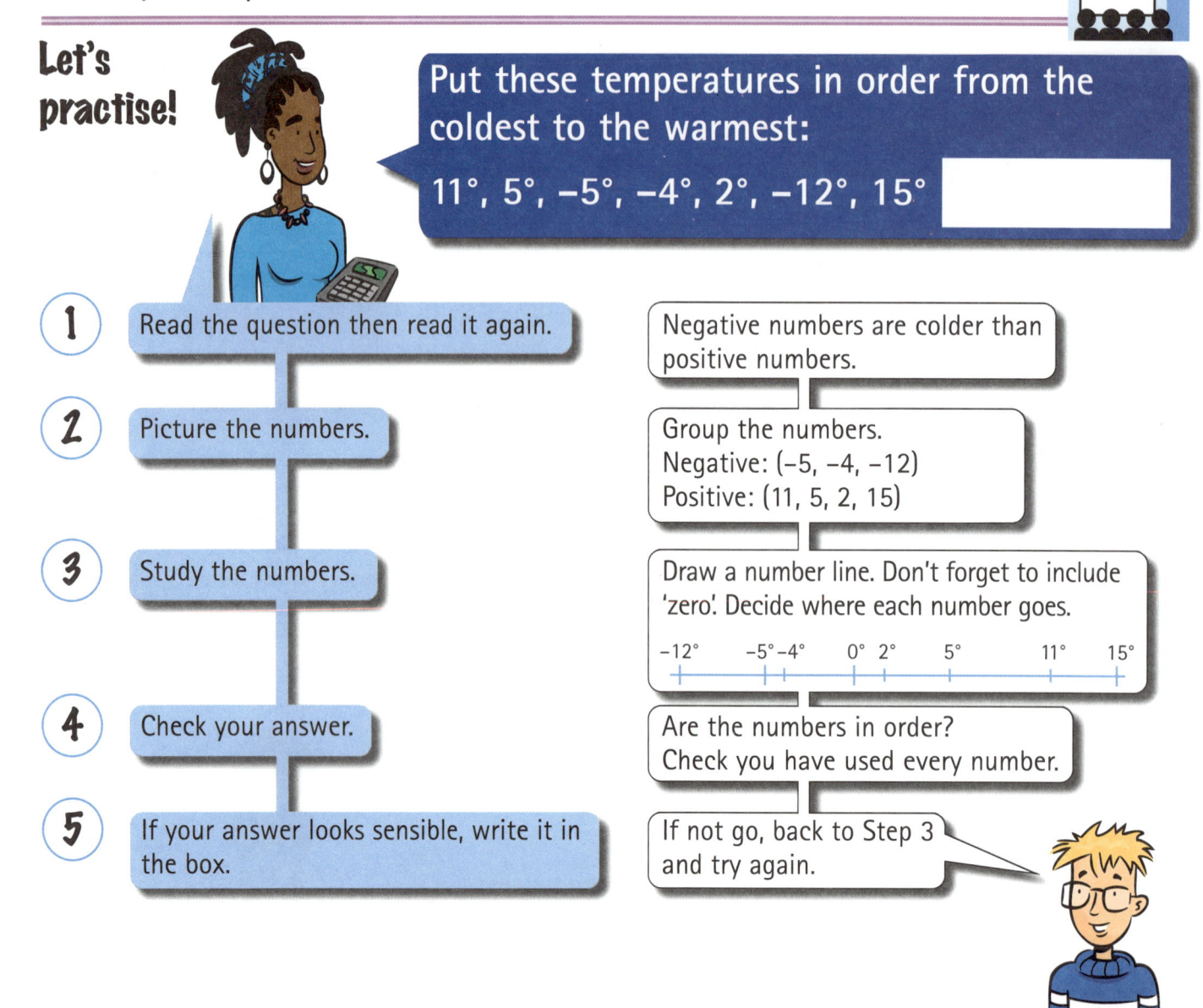

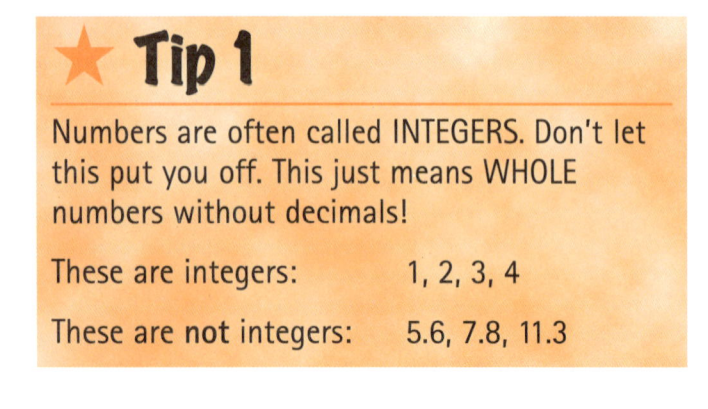

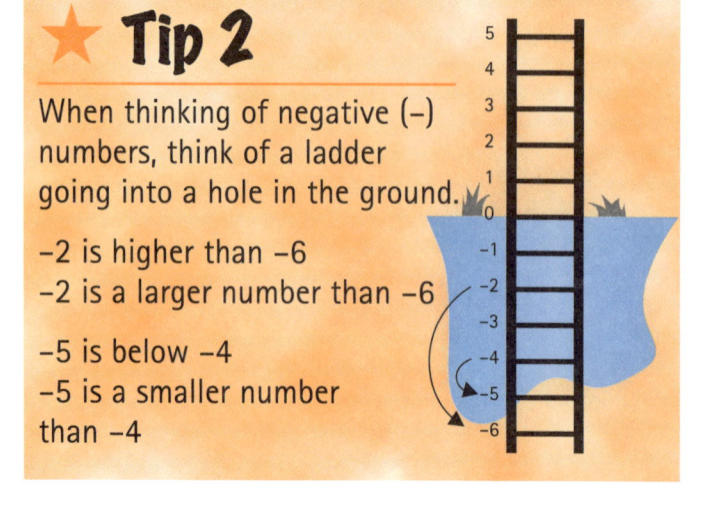

Let's practise!

Put these temperatures in order from the coldest to the warmest:

11°, 5°, −5°, −4°, 2°, −12°, 15°

1. Read the question then read it again. → Negative numbers are colder than positive numbers.

2. Picture the numbers. → Group the numbers.
   Negative: (−5, −4, −12)
   Positive: (11, 5, 2, 15)

3. Study the numbers. → Draw a number line. Don't forget to include 'zero'. Decide where each number goes.

   −12°   −5° −4°   0° 2°   5°   11°   15°

4. Check your answer. → Are the numbers in order? Check you have used every number.

5. If your answer looks sensible, write it in the box. → If not go, back to Step 3 and try again.

★ Tip 1

Numbers are often called INTEGERS. Don't let this put you off. This just means WHOLE numbers without decimals!

These are integers: 1, 2, 3, 4

These are **not** integers: 5.6, 7.8, 11.3

★ Tip 2

When thinking of negative (−) numbers, think of a ladder going into a hole in the ground.

−2 is higher than −6
−2 is a larger number than −6

−5 is below −4
−5 is a smaller number than −4

THE NUMBER SYSTEM AND CALCULATIONS 25

Try another question. This time it's a word problem.

Let's practise!

The temperature is −9°. It rises by 14°. What is the new temperature?

1. Read the question then read it again.
2. Picture the numbers.
3. Calculate your answer.
4. Check your answer.
5. If your answer checks out, write it in the box.

Rises means getting warmer.

−9° is colder than 14°.

−9 −8 −7 −6 −5 −4 −3 −2 −1 0 1 2 3 4 5 6 7 8 9 10

The temperature starts at −9°. We then need to count up 14 places.

Did you count in the right direction? When adding to a negative number always count towards zero.

Our answer is 5° which is 14° warmer than −9°! Brrr…

−25−24−23−22−21−20−19−18−17−16−15−14−13−12−11−10−9 −8 −7 −6 −5 −4 −3 −2 −1 −0 1 2 3 4 5 6 7 8 9 10 11 12 13 14 15 16 17 18 19 20 21 22 23 24 25

Practice questions
Use the number line to help you.

1. Put these temperatures in order, lowest to highest:
   −1°, 3°, 0°, 2°, −4°

2. Order these integers starting with the smallest:
   −5, −25, −3, −17, 17, −11

3. At 6pm the temperature is 5°. Once the sun sets at 6.30pm the temperature falls to 3°. The temperature then drops by 2° every hour until 11.30pm.
   What will the temperature be at 11.30pm?

4. If the temperature at the top of a mountain is −25° on Monday and rises 6° every day, what will the temperature be by Saturday?

Simple formulae

Achieved?

Formulae can be written in words or in letters. To achieve Level 5 you may be required to make up your own formulae in the tests. This is easier than it sounds! Let's start by working through this example.

Let's practise!

Here is a formula for finding the total cost of a pay-as-you-go mobile phone call.
T = £0.25 × N   T = total cost
Each minute costs 25p
N = number of minutes

Now write a formula for finding the cost of one call when the total cost of N calls is £2.25 and the cost of one call is C.

1 Read the question then read it again.

Lots to read and think about here!

2 What am I being asked to do?

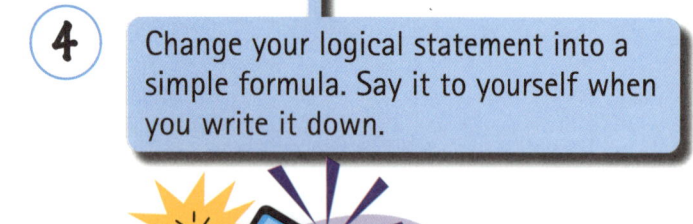

Write a formula for finding the cost of one call using £2.25, and 'N' and 'C'.

3 It will help if you say the formula to yourself.

The total cost is £2.25. So... the cost of one call is £2.25, divided by the number of calls, N.

4 Change your logical statement into a simple formula. Say it to yourself when you write it down.

The cost of one minute...	C
... is the total cost...	£2.25
... divided by (÷) the total number of calls	N

C = £2.25 ÷ N   OR
C = £2.25
       N

★ Tip 1
★ Talk through your formula in your head.
★ Think clearly.
★ Take it step-by-step.

★ Tip 2
It helps to only use letters that relate to the information in the question, e.g. C = Cost.

THE NUMBER SYSTEM AND CALCULATIONS

A simple formula is often used to find out the total cost of items bought. In words this formula can be written:

"The total cost is the price of one item multiplied by the number of those items bought."

In letter formulae this could be written as: T = N × P

T = total cost   P = price of each item   N = number of items bought

Practice questions
Use the T = N × P formula to work out these questions.

1. What is the value of T if N = 8 and P = £1.75?
2. What is the value of N if T = £60 and P = £3? **20**
3. What is the value of P if T = £72 and N = 9?

Example question
James and Melissa are playing a number game. James gives Melissa a number which she changes using a rule:

"I take James's number and multiply it by 9 then subtract 8."

Write a formula to show the process Melissa goes through to get to her answer.

Use J for James's number and M for Melissa's answer.

M = (J × 9) − 8

Practice question
Now Melissa changes the rule:

"I take James's number and multiply it by 7 then add 7."

Write a formula to show the process Melissa goes through to get to her answer. Use J for James's number and M for Melissa's answer.

M =

★ Tip
If a number and a letter are next to each other, e.g. 4N, it means they are multiplied. Why is the × (multiply) symbol left out? Because it could get confused with the letter x!!

Using brackets

Achieved? 😊 😐 ☹

To achieve Level 5 in Maths you must be able to answer questions that contain brackets. Let's look at a simple example.

Firstly, a sum without brackets might look like this:

$5 \times 4 + 7 = 27$

If brackets are used then the answer changes:

$5 \times (4 + 7) = 55$

> CALCULATIONS INSIDE BRACKETS MUST BE DONE FIRST!
>
> Our second example actually becomes $5 \times 11 = 55$ when we calculate the brackets first.

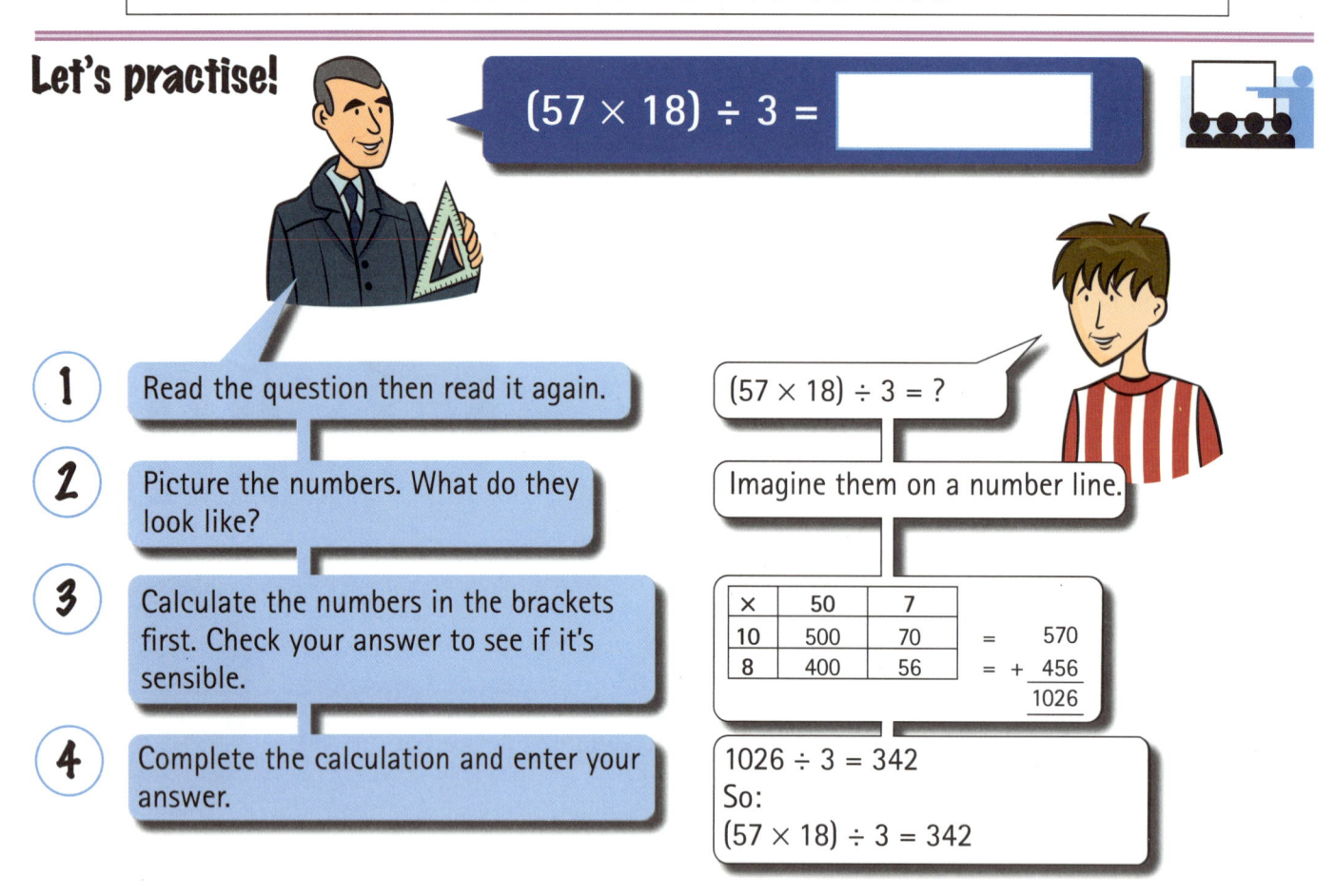

Let's practise!

$(57 \times 18) \div 3 = \boxed{}$

1. Read the question then read it again.

   $(57 \times 18) \div 3 = ?$

2. Picture the numbers. What do they look like?

   Imagine them on a number line.

3. Calculate the numbers in the brackets first. Check your answer to see if it's sensible.

×	50	7
10	500	70
8	400	56

   $= 570$
   $= + 456$
   $\overline{1026}$

4. Complete the calculation and enter your answer.

   $1026 \div 3 = 342$
   So:
   $(57 \times 18) \div 3 = 342$

★ Tip

Brackets are very sensitive and need your attention.

ALWAYS CALCULATE THE BRACKETS FIRST!

THE NUMBER SYSTEM AND CALCULATIONS 29

Here is another question with brackets that we can do together. Try the practice questions at the bottom when you think you're ready.

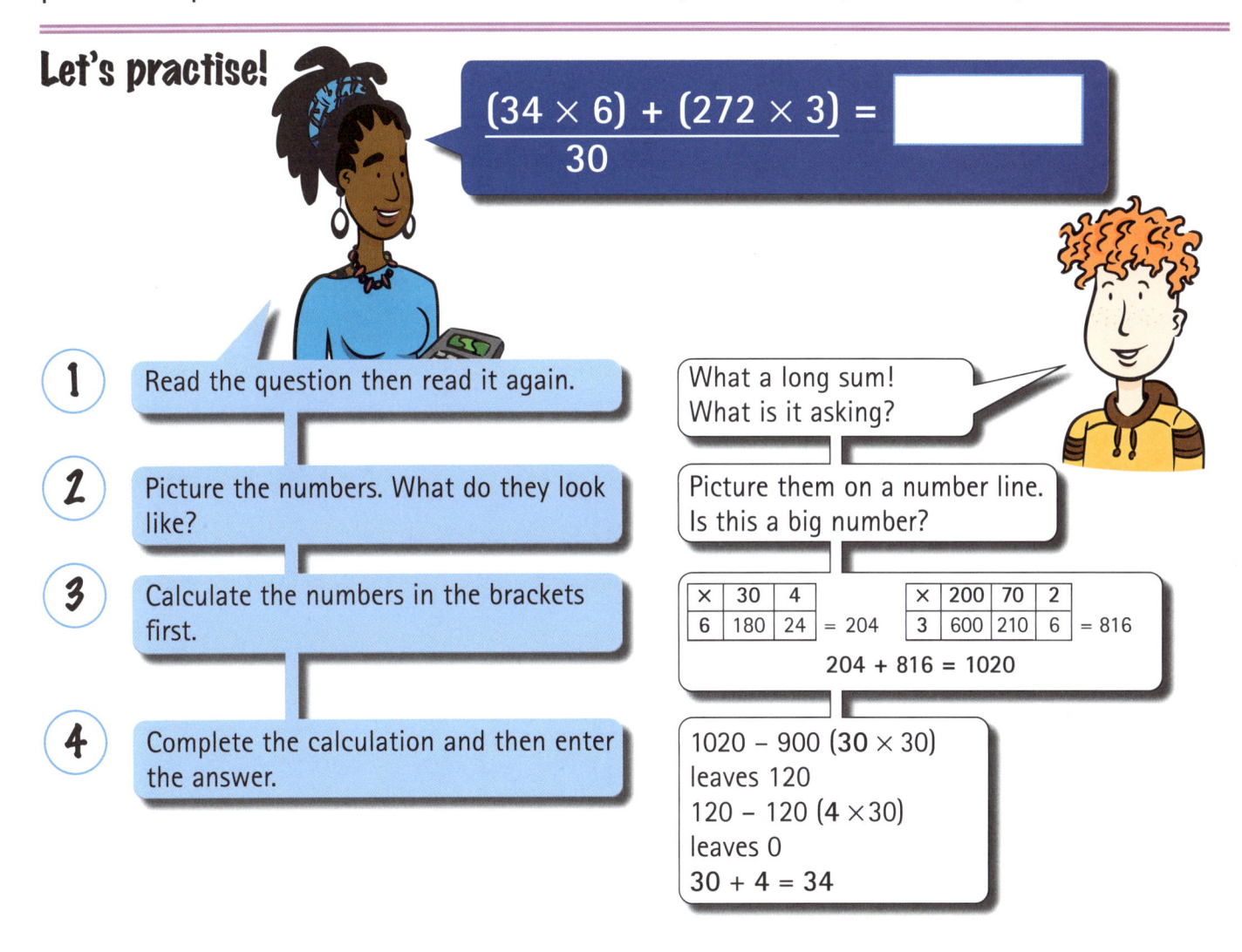

Let's practise!

$$\frac{(34 \times 6) + (272 \times 3)}{30} = \boxed{}$$

① Read the question then read it again.

② Picture the numbers. What do they look like?

③ Calculate the numbers in the brackets first.

④ Complete the calculation and then enter the answer.

What a long sum! What is it asking?

Picture them on a number line. Is this a big number?

×	30	4
6	180	24	= 204

×	200	70	2
3	600	210	6	= 816

204 + 816 = 1020

1020 − 900 (30 × 30) leaves 120
120 − 120 (4 × 30) leaves 0
30 + 4 = 34

Practice questions

Here are some questions for you to try. Remember to use the step-by-step approach above.

① $82 \times (39 + 66) = \boxed{}$

② $(75 \times 38) + 682 = \boxed{}$

③ $(23 \times 97) + \boxed{} = 5000$

④ $(22 \times 33) + \boxed{} = 4444$

⑤ $\dfrac{(61 \times 48) - (72 \times 21)}{6} = \boxed{}$

⑥ $\dfrac{(88 \times 31) - (42 \times 58)}{4} = \boxed{}$

Coordinates

Achieved?

To achieve Level 5 you should be familiar with coordinates and quadrants. Let's try a question to practise what we know!

Let's practise!

Write down the coordinates of each point on this graph.

1st quadrant = (_ , _)
2nd quadrant = (_ , _)
3rd quadrant = (_ , _)
4th quadrant = (_ , _)

Remember which quadrant is which!

2nd	1st
3rd	4th

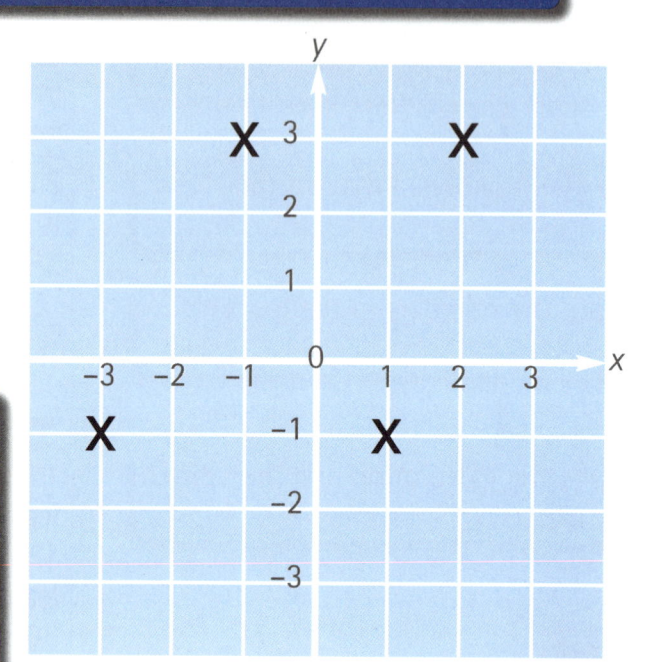

1. Read the question then read it again.

2. Practise your answer.

3. Check the number of each quadrant.

You can sketch in lines to help you read the coordinates.

2nd quadrant	1st quadrant
3rd quadrant	4th quadrant

4. Read off the coordinates in each quadrant.

Remember, read:
ALONG the x axis first, then **UP** or **DOWN** the y axis.
1 (2, 3)   2 (−1, 3)
3 (−3, −1)   4 (1, −1)

5. Double-check and write in your answer.

Check twice! Write once!

MEASURES, SHAPE AND SPACE 31

Let's try another question.

Using the y axis as a mirror line, draw a reflection of the pentagon in the 1st quadrant.

Write the new coordinates of each vertex here

(_ , _)
(_ , _)
(_ , _)
(_ , _)
(_ , _)

1. Read the question then read it again.

2. Practise your answer.

3. Note the position of your shape.

4. Draw your shape on the grid above.

5. Read off your coordinates.

6. Double-check and write in the answer.

Note you are being asked to work in the 1st quadrant. 'vertex = corner'.

Sketch your pentagon on rough paper first.

Your pentagon must go in the 1st quadrant, mirrored in the y axis!

Remember, read along then UP/DOWN: (3, 0), (4, 0), (4, 1), (3, 2), (2, 1).

Check twice! Write once!

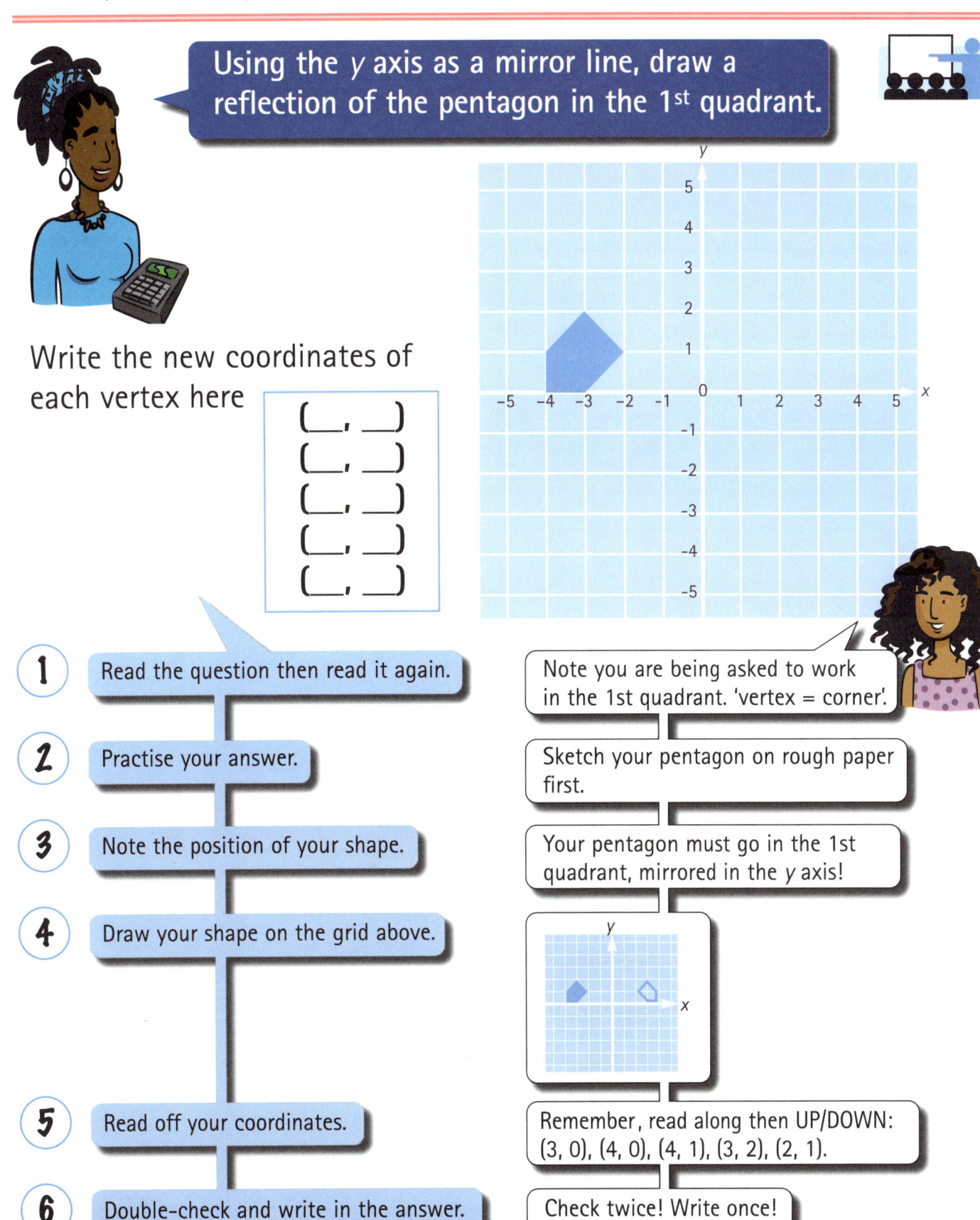

When you feel comfortable with this, try the practice questions over the page...

Practice questions

1 In which quadrants will we find:

(−1, 4)   (5, −3)   (3, 1)   (−2, −1)

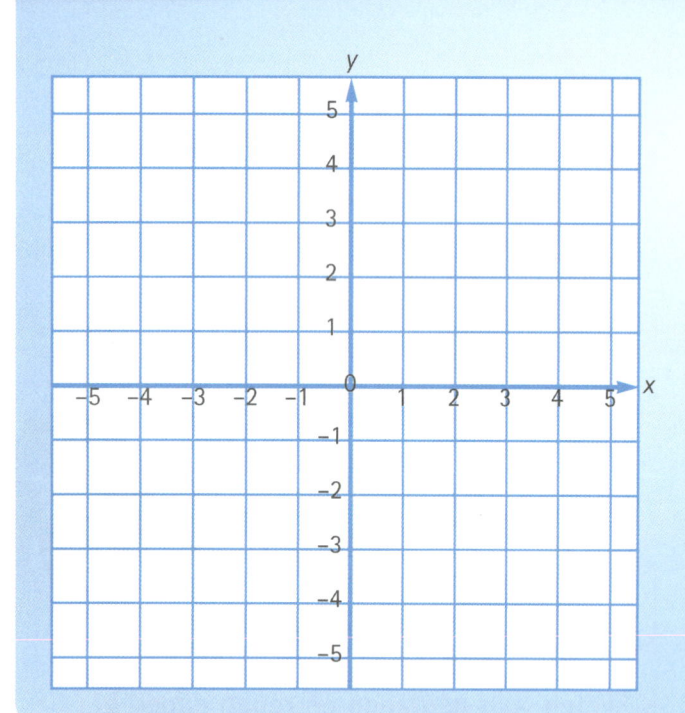

☐   ☐   ☐   ☐

2 Draw a reflection of the parallelogram in the x axis. Name the coordinates of the reflected shape.

(_, _) (_, _) (_, _) (_, _)

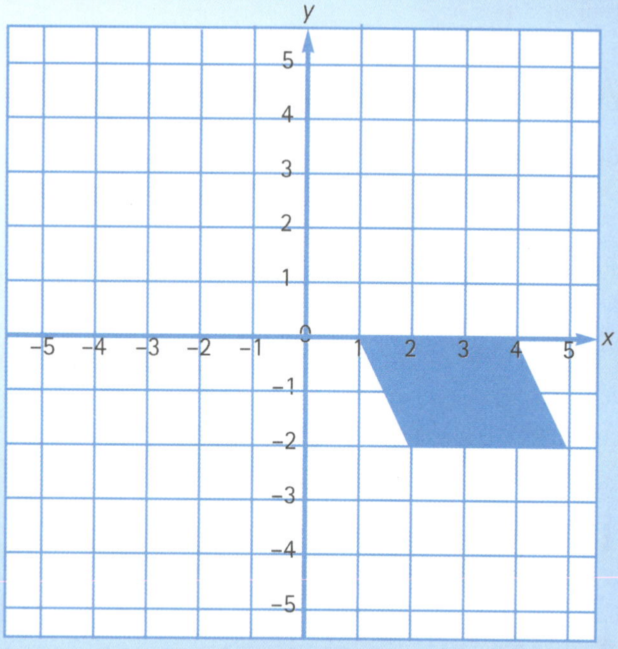

★ Tip 1

Coordinates always go ALONG the corridor and UP the stairs.

But Miss, you can go DOWN stairs as well!

Always go along first when reading coordinates. x (axis) comes before y (axis)!

★ Tip 2

Coordinates are always written in brackets.
(3, 4)   (−3, −2)
or
(x axis, y axis)

★ Tip 3

The coordinates plot where the grid lines cross, not the space in between them.

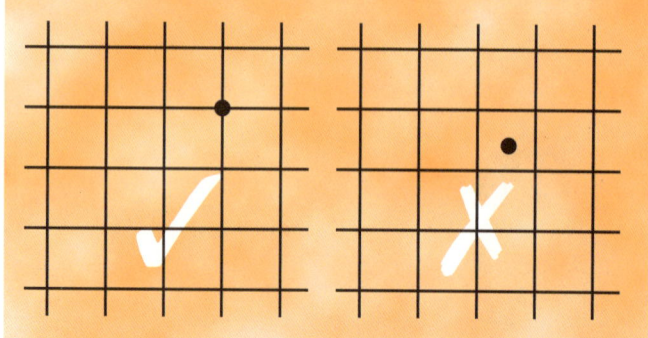

MEASURES, SHAPE AND SPACE 33

Angles

Achieved? 😊 😐 ☹

To achieve Level 5 you will need to be able to measure and draw angles and use the correct language for them.

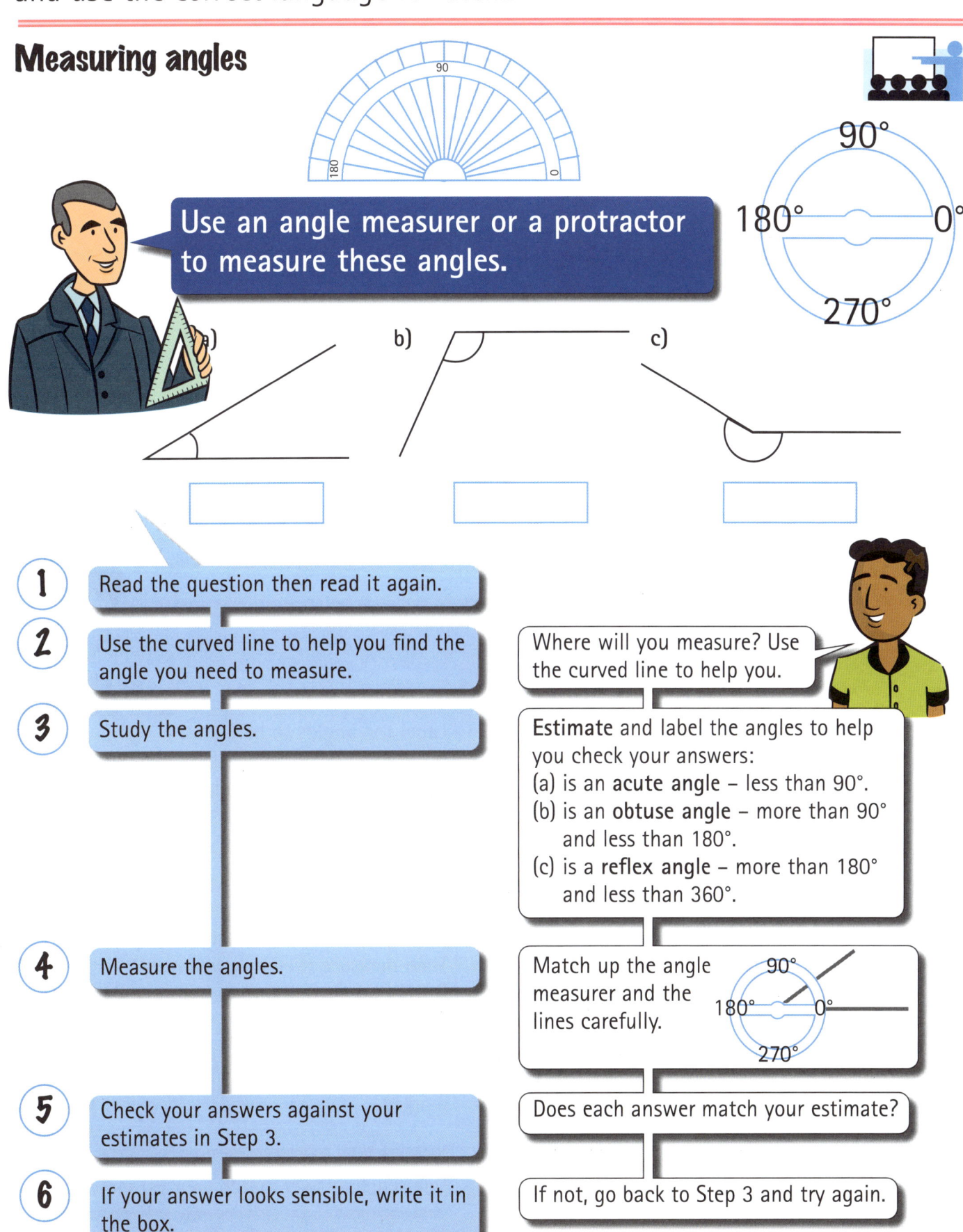

Measuring angles

Use an angle measurer or a protractor to measure these angles.

a)   b)   c)

| 1 | Read the question then read it again. |

| 2 | Use the curved line to help you find the angle you need to measure. |

Where will you measure? Use the curved line to help you.

| 3 | Study the angles. |

Estimate and label the angles to help you check your answers:
(a) is an **acute angle** – less than 90°.
(b) is an **obtuse angle** – more than 90° and less than 180°.
(c) is a **reflex angle** – more than 180° and less than 360°.

| 4 | Measure the angles. |

Match up the angle measurer and the lines carefully.

| 5 | Check your answers against your estimates in Step 3. |

Does each answer match your estimate?

| 6 | If your answer looks sensible, write it in the box. |

If not, go back to Step 3 and try again.

MEASURES, SHAPE AND SPACE

Drawing angles

Let's try drawing some angles. Use some paper to practise.

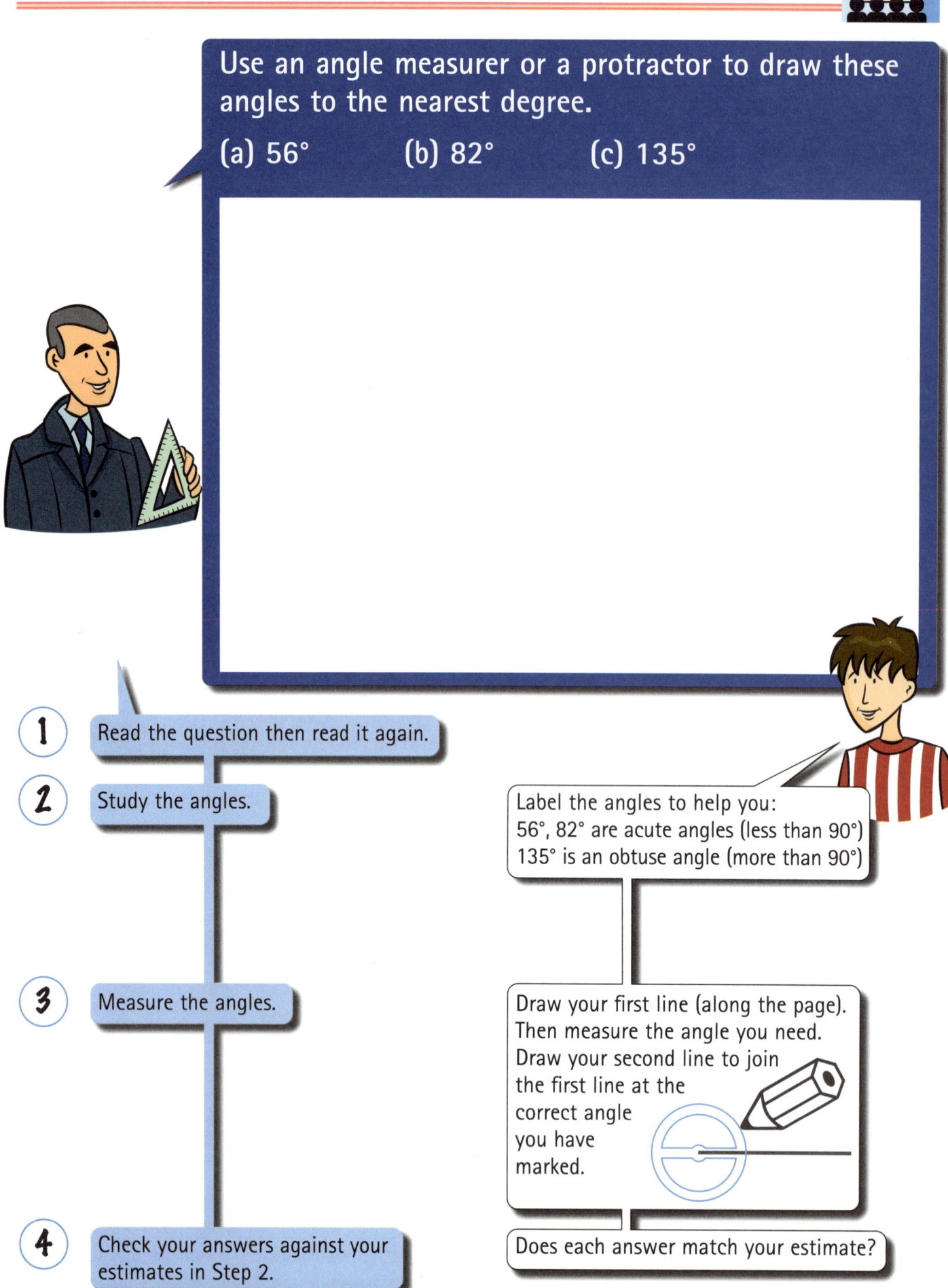

Use an angle measurer or a protractor to draw these angles to the nearest degree.

(a) 56°   (b) 82°   (c) 135°

1. Read the question then read it again.

2. Study the angles.

Label the angles to help you:
56°, 82° are acute angles (less than 90°)
135° is an obtuse angle (more than 90°)

3. Measure the angles.

Draw your first line (along the page). Then measure the angle you need. Draw your second line to join the first line at the correct angle you have marked.

4. Check your answers against your estimates in Step 2.

Does each answer match your estimate?

MEASURES, SHAPE AND SPACE 35

To achieve Level 5 you also need to be able to measure or work out the size of the angles in a triangle and at a point.

Just remember: angles in a triangle add up to 180°.

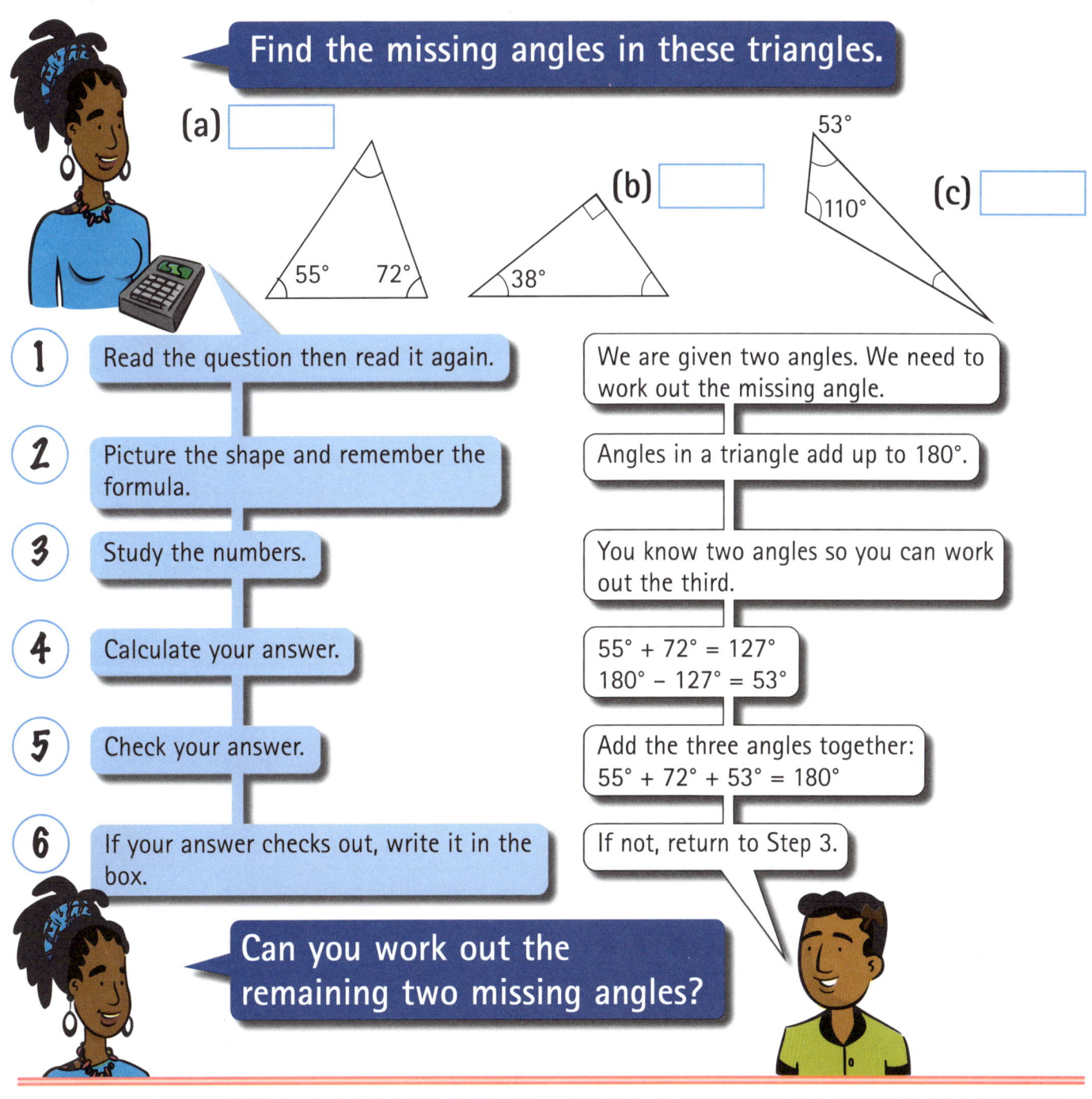

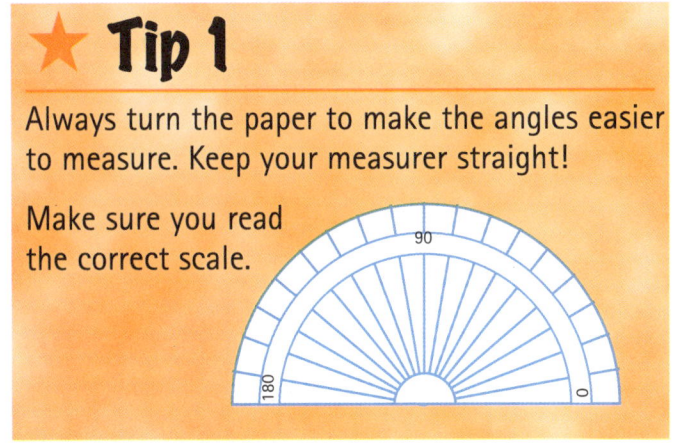

Find the missing angles in these triangles.

(a) ☐   (b) ☐   (c) ☐

Triangle (a): 55°, 72°
Triangle (b): 38°, right angle
Triangle (c): 53°, 110°

1. Read the question then read it again.
2. Picture the shape and remember the formula.
3. Study the numbers.
4. Calculate your answer.
5. Check your answer.
6. If your answer checks out, write it in the box.

- We are given two angles. We need to work out the missing angle.
- Angles in a triangle add up to 180°.
- You know two angles so you can work out the third.
- 55° + 72° = 127°
  180° − 127° = 53°
- Add the three angles together:
  55° + 72° + 53° = 180°
- If not, return to Step 3.

Can you work out the remaining two missing angles?

★ Tip 1
Always turn the paper to make the angles easier to measure. Keep your measurer straight!

Make sure you read the correct scale.

★ Tip 2
Think of a darts board to help you remember the angles in a triangle.

One hundred and EIGHTYYYYY!

Angles at a point

Let's practise!

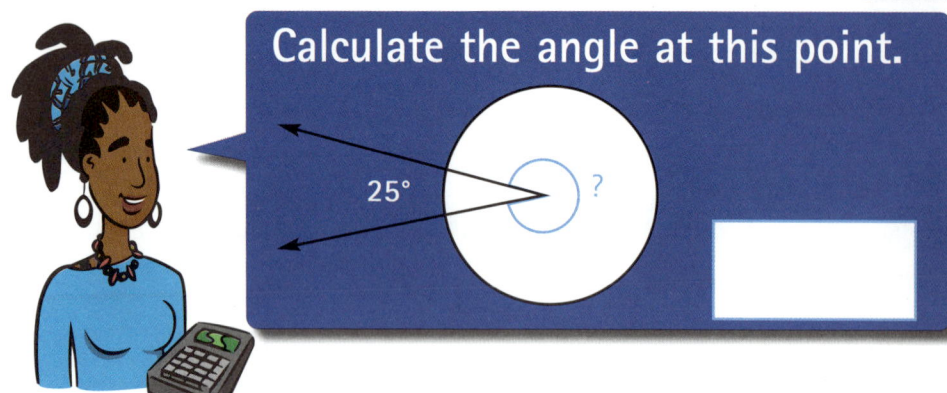

Calculate the angle at this point.

25° ?

1. Read the question then read it again. — 'Calculate' usually means you need to do a sum to work out the answer!
2. Picture the shape. Estimate the angle. — The angle is between 180° and 360°.
3. Remember the formula. — A complete turn = 360°.
4. Study the numbers. — You know one angle so you can work out the other.
5. Calculate your answer. — 360° − 25° = 335°
6. Check your answer. — Does it match your estimate?
7. If your answer checks out, write it in the box. — If not, return to Step 4.

★ Tip 1

A complete turn = 360°

Imagine a skateboarder turning right around.

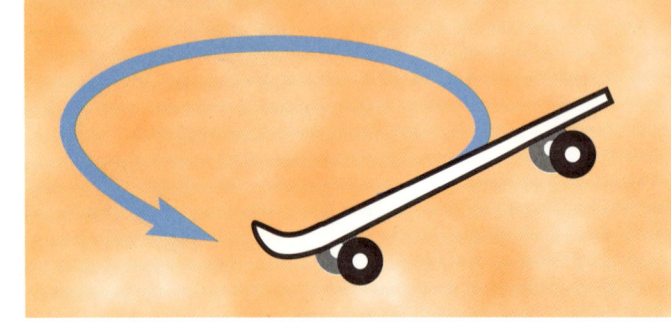

★ Tip 2

A right angle is always shown by a box.

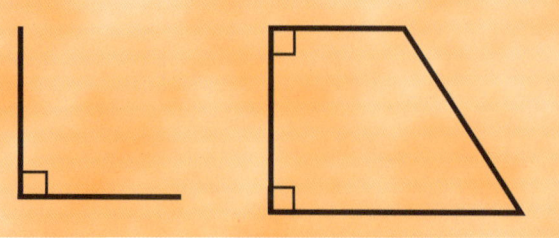

Practice questions

1 Find the missing angles in these triangles.

(a) [triangle with 67° and right angle] → [ ]

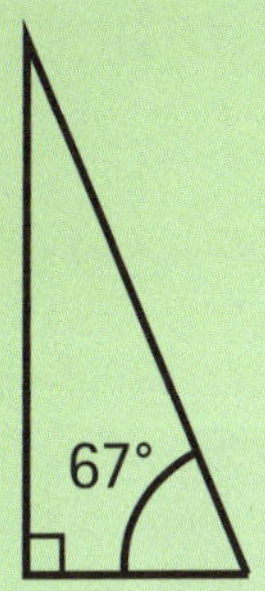

(b) [triangle with 110° and 30°] → [ ]

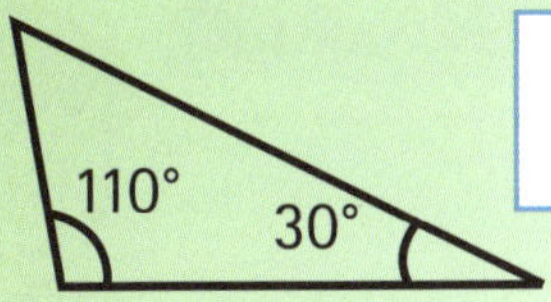

(c) [triangle with 78° and 35°] → [ ]

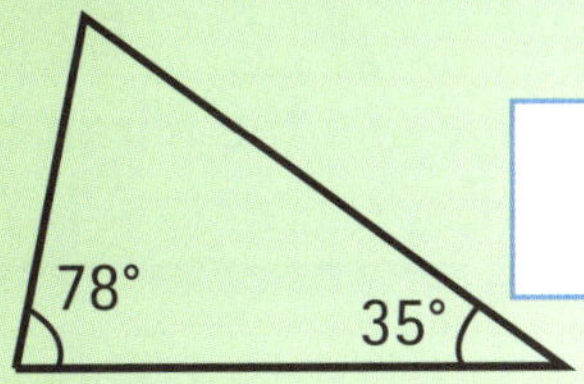

2 Find the angle at each point.

(a) [angle marked ? with 84° shown] → [ ]

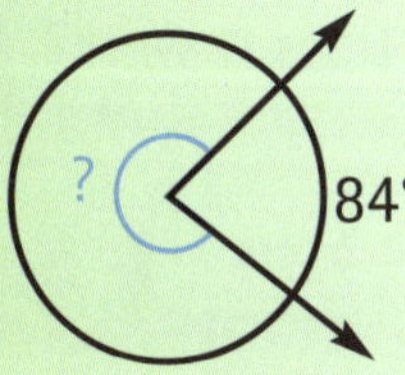

(b) [angle marked ? with 125° shown] → [ ]

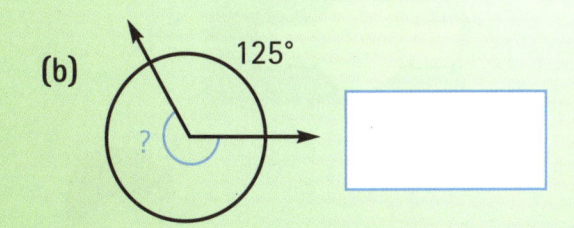

(c) [angle marked ? with 33° shown] → [ ]

3 Estimate the size of these angles. Then label them acute, reflex, obtuse or right.

(a) [right angle] (b) [obtuse angle]

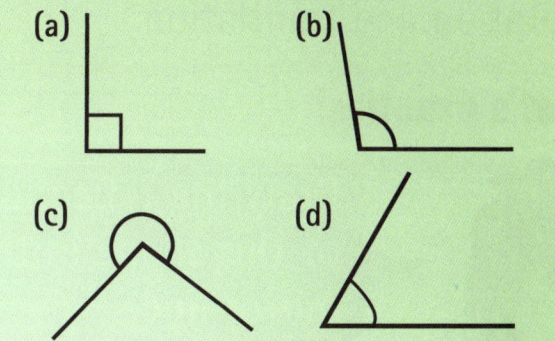

(c) [reflex angle] (d) [acute angle]

(a) [ ]

(b) [ ]

(c) [ ]

(d) [ ]

4 Draw an angle of 75° to the nearest degree.

[ ]

5 Measure this angle to the nearest degree.

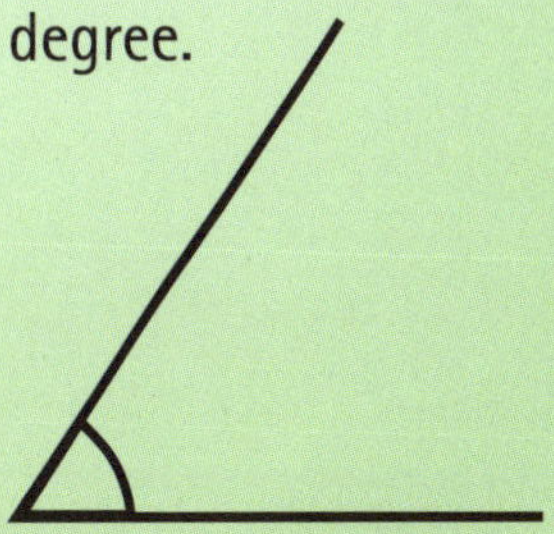

[ ]

38 MEASURES, SHAPE AND SPACE

Symmetries of 2D shapes

Achieved? 😊 😐 ☹

To achieve Level 5 in Maths you will need to understand reflection, rotation and translation.

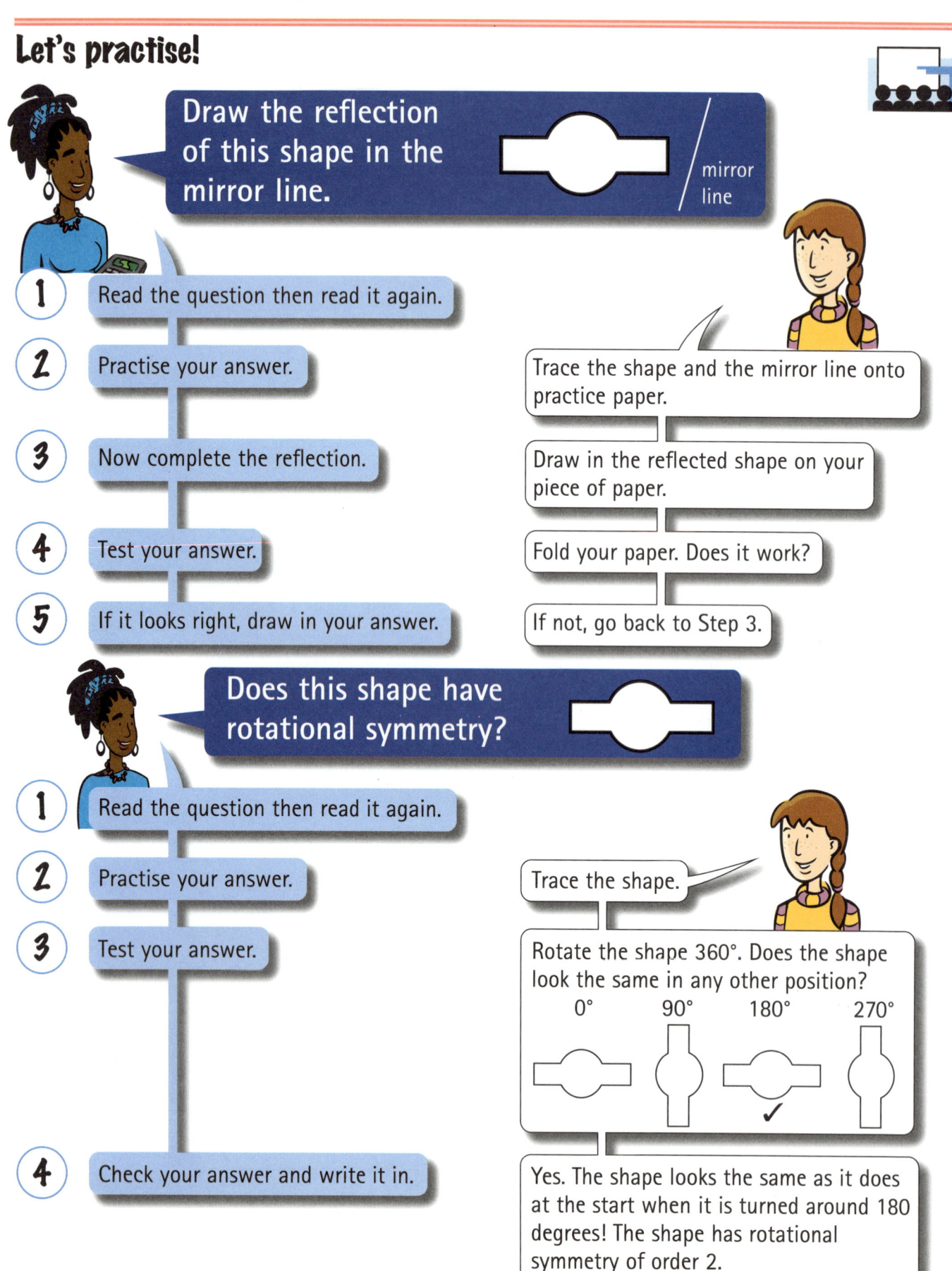

Let's practise!

Draw the reflection of this shape in the mirror line.

mirror line

1. Read the question then read it again.
2. Practise your answer.
   - Trace the shape and the mirror line onto practice paper.
3. Now complete the reflection.
   - Draw in the reflected shape on your piece of paper.
4. Test your answer.
   - Fold your paper. Does it work?
5. If it looks right, draw in your answer.
   - If not, go back to Step 3.

Does this shape have rotational symmetry?

1. Read the question then read it again.
2. Practise your answer.
   - Trace the shape.
3. Test your answer.
   - Rotate the shape 360°. Does the shape look the same in any other position?
     - 0° 90° 180° ✓ 270°
4. Check your answer and write it in.
   - Yes. The shape looks the same as it does at the start when it is turned around 180 degrees! The shape has rotational symmetry of order 2.

MEASURES, SHAPE AND SPACE 39

Let's try a question about translation now.

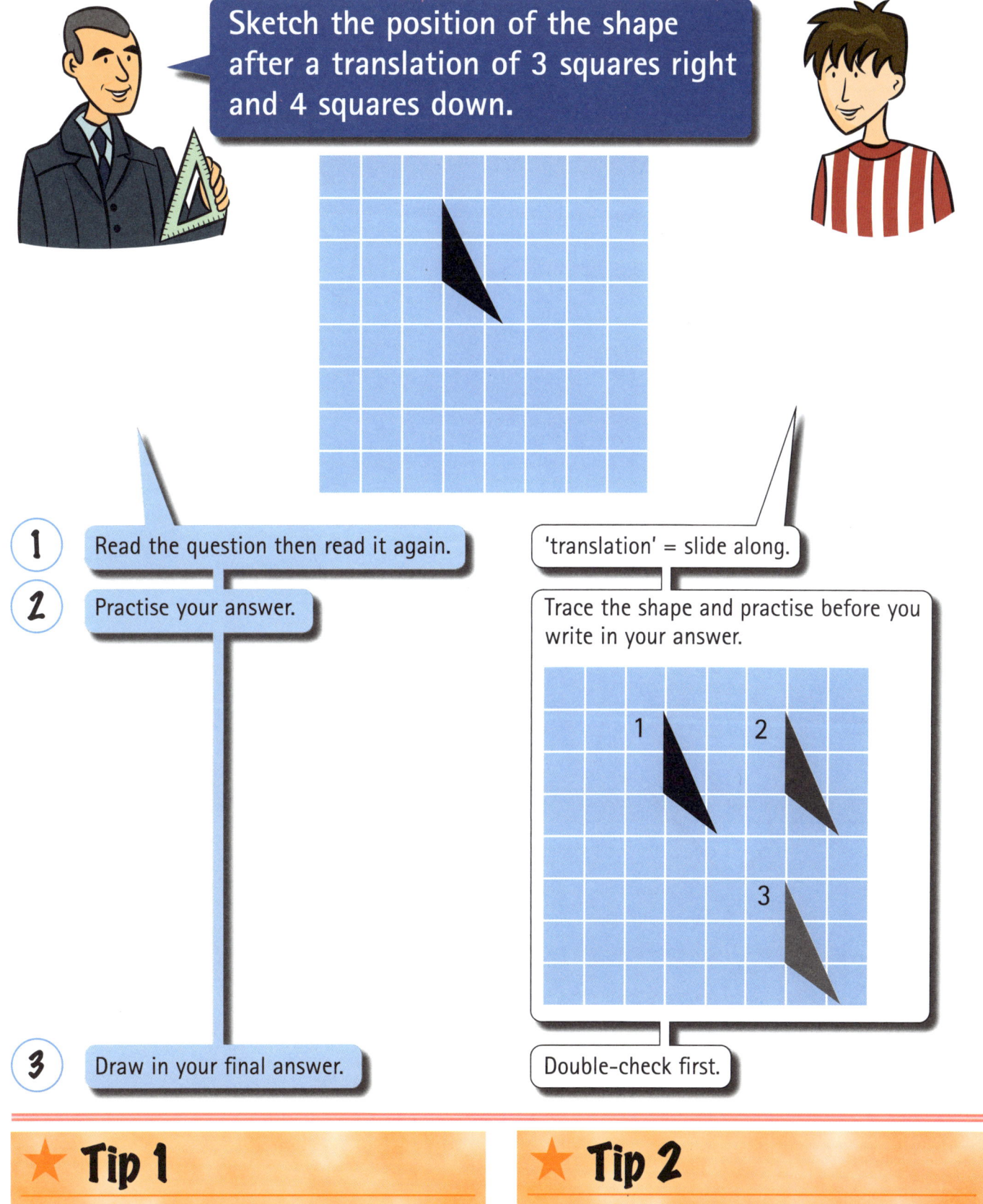

> Sketch the position of the shape after a translation of 3 squares right and 4 squares down.

① Read the question then read it again.

② Practise your answer.

'translation' = slide along.

Trace the shape and practise before you write in your answer.

Double-check first.

③ Draw in your final answer.

★ Tip 1
If there is no grid given, then trace the object and give it a base.

★ Tip 2
Translation means 'slide along'. It is not the same as rotation, which means 'turn around'.

★ Tip 3
The order of rotational symmetry is the number of times you can turn a shape through 360° and it looks the same as the original. 0° 90° 180° 270° The oval has rotational symmetry of order 2.

40 MEASURES, SHAPE AND SPACE

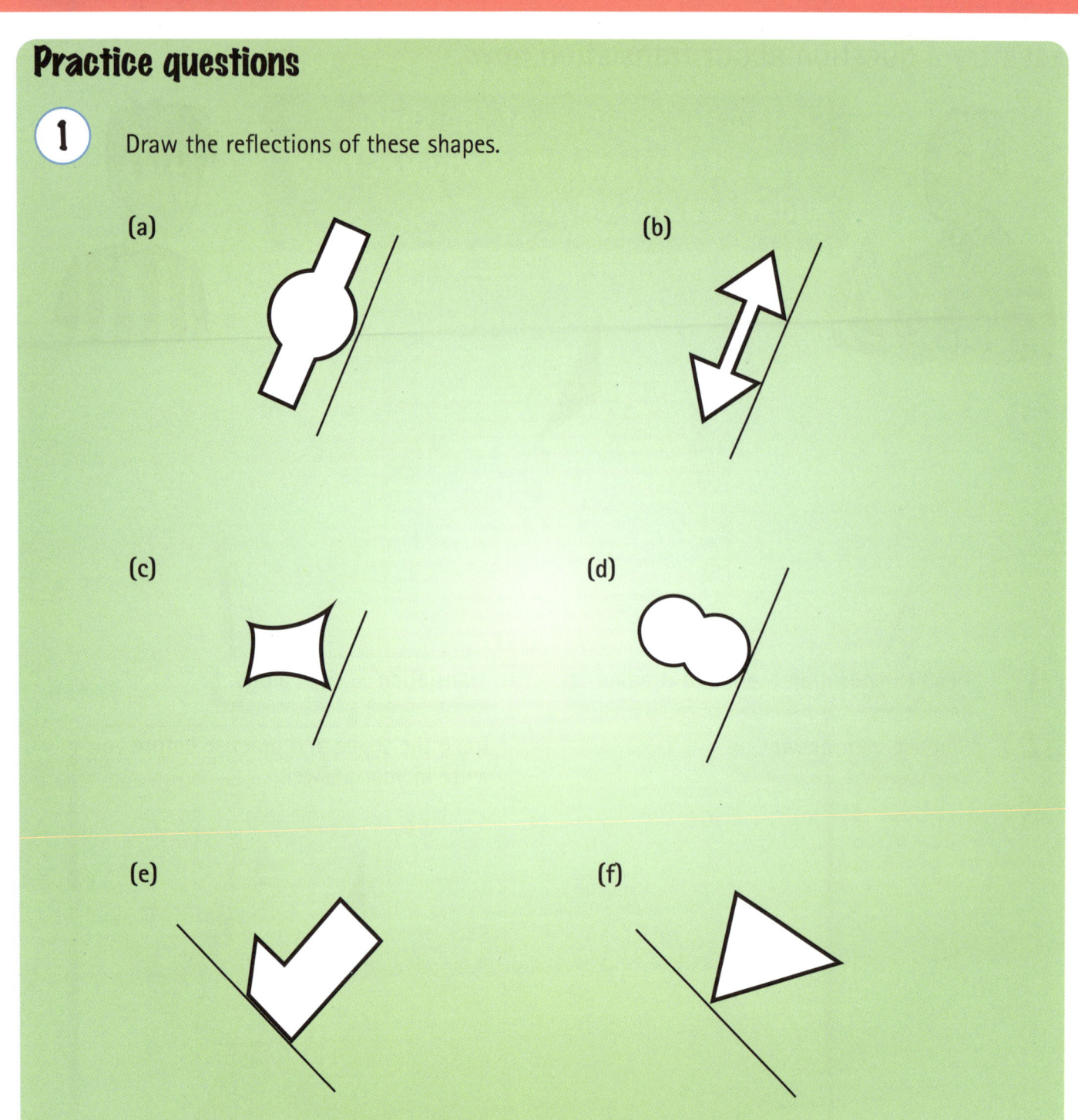

Practice questions

1 Draw the reflections of these shapes.

(a)

(b)

(c)

(d)

(e)

(f)

★ Tip 1
Lines of symmetry = mirror lines

★ Tip 2
Don't let your paper slip!

Practice questions

2 Which of these shapes have rotational symmetry? Tick those that do and write their order.

(a) [ladybird] (b) [rhombus with cross] (c) Z (d) [flower]

3 Tick the correctly translated shapes.

(a) (b)

(c) (d)

(e) (f)

Units of measure

Comparing metric to imperial units of measure

To achieve Level 5 you will have to answer questions that ask you to compare metric units of measurement (kilometres, grams, litres and centimetres) with imperial units of measurement (miles, pounds, pints). Look at the conversions in the Key Facts on page 61.

Try this one.

Write 75 kg as grams.

1. Read the question then read it again.
2. Study the units.
3. Calculate the answer.
4. Add in the correct units.
5. If your answer looks sensible, write it in the box.

75 kg = ? g

1 kg = 1000 g

75 × 1000 = 75 000

75 000 g

If not, go back to Step 2 and try again.

Practice questions

Here are some questions. Use the Key Facts on page 61 to help you.

1. My little brother is 38 inches tall. How many centimetres is that?

☐ cm

2. My little sister only weighs 40 lbs. How many kgs is that?

☐ kg

★ Tip

Revision rhymes!

A metre is just 3 feet 3. It's longer than a yard you see!

2 and a bit pounds of jam is round about 1 kilo of ham!

MEASURES, SHAPE AND SPACE 43

To achieve Level 5 you will have to answer questions that ask you to convert one metric unit to another metric unit.

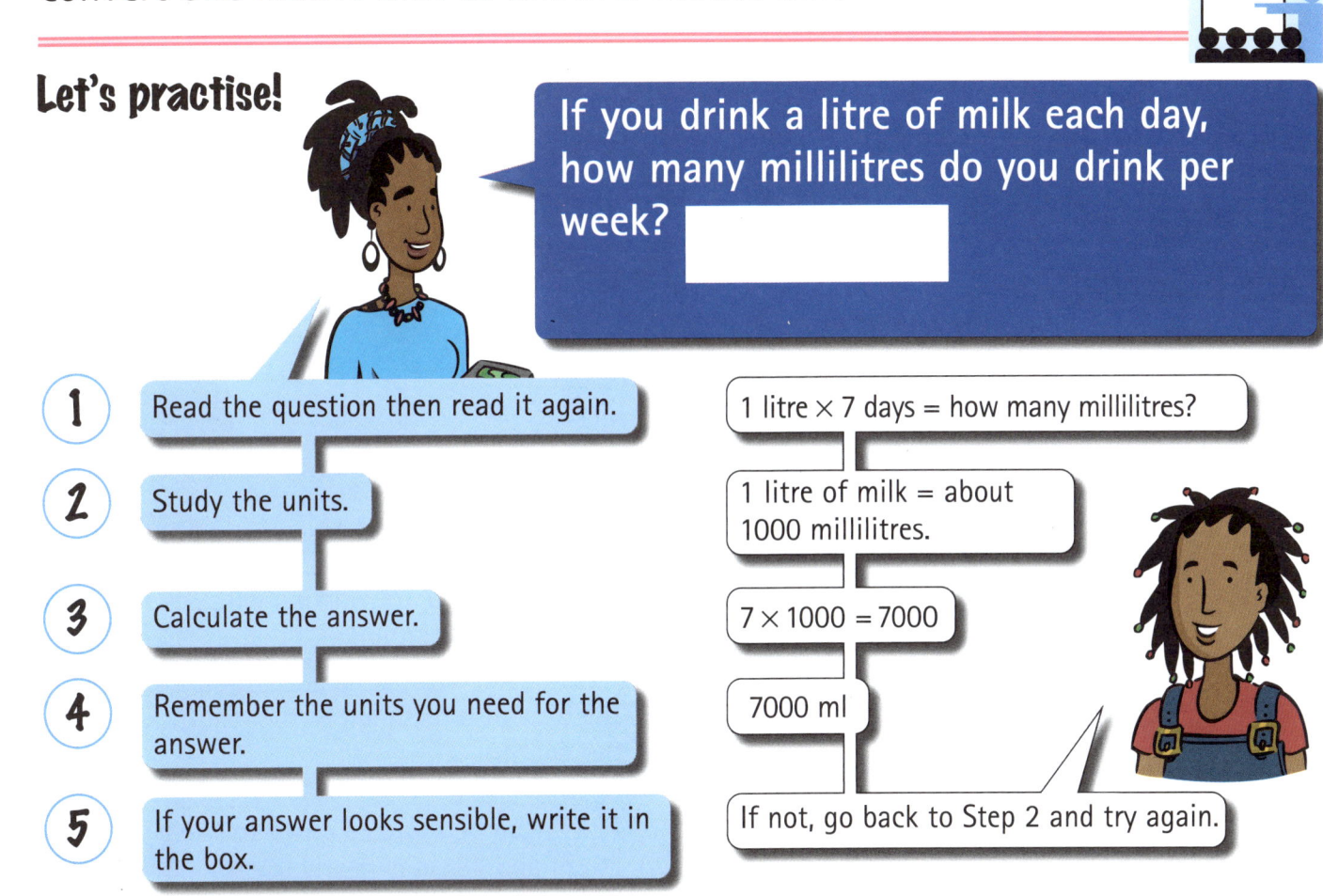

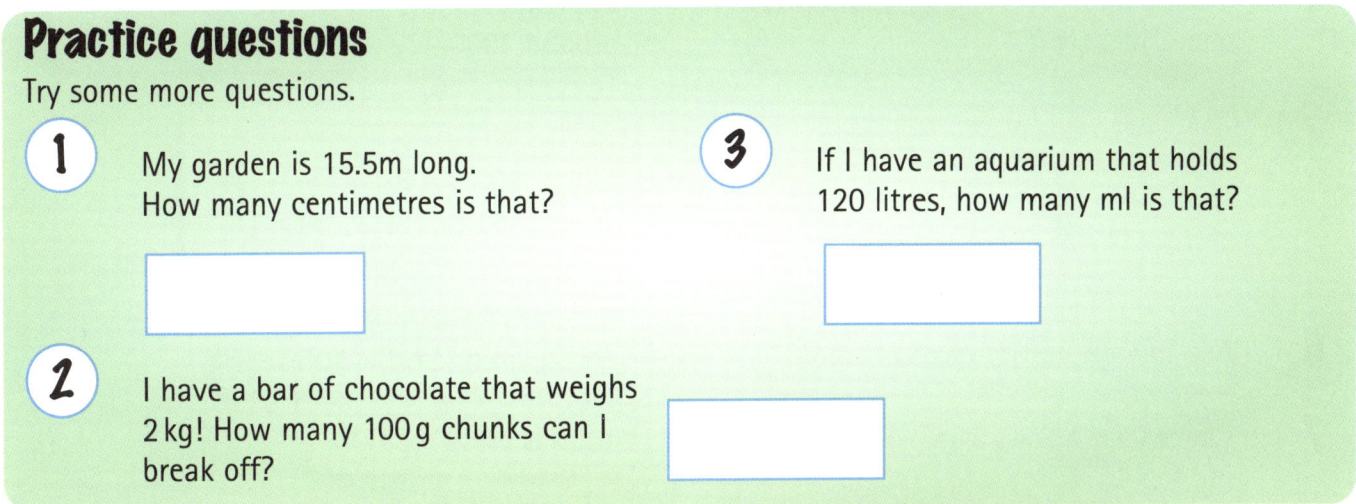

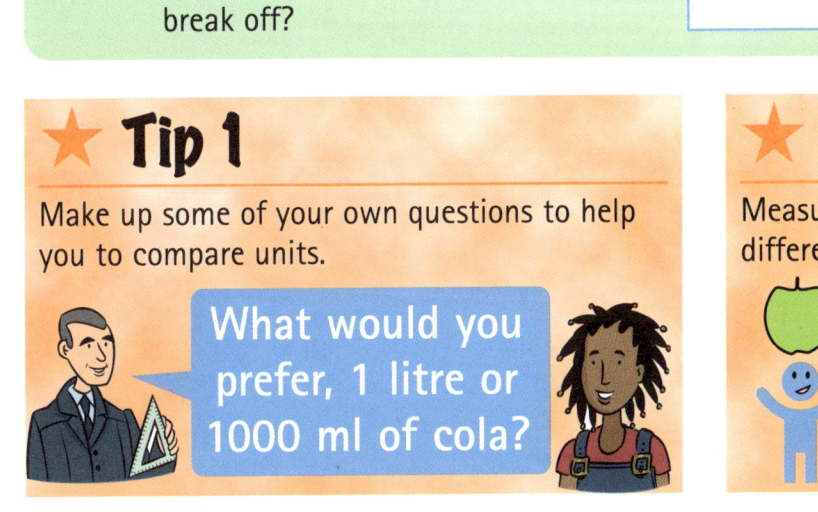

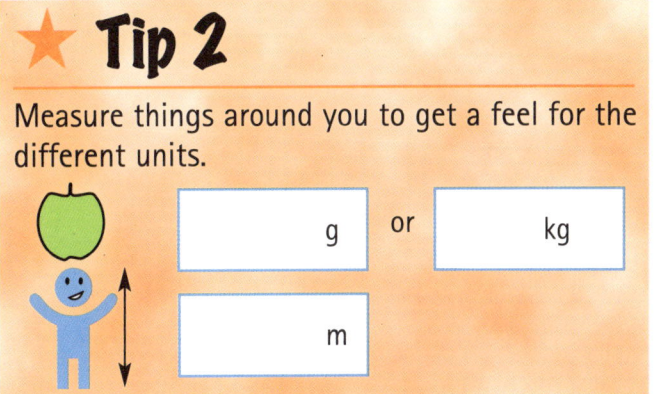

Let's practise!

If you drink a litre of milk each day, how many millilitres do you drink per week?

1. Read the question then read it again.
2. Study the units.
3. Calculate the answer.
4. Remember the units you need for the answer.
5. If your answer looks sensible, write it in the box.

1 litre × 7 days = how many millilitres?

1 litre of milk = about 1000 millilitres.

7 × 1000 = 7000

7000 ml

If not, go back to Step 2 and try again.

Practice questions

Try some more questions.

1. My garden is 15.5m long. How many centimetres is that?

2. I have a bar of chocolate that weighs 2 kg! How many 100g chunks can I break off?

3. If I have an aquarium that holds 120 litres, how many ml is that?

★ Tip 1
Make up some of your own questions to help you to compare units.

What would you prefer, 1 litre or 1000 ml of cola?

★ Tip 2
Measure things around you to get a feel for the different units.

g   or   kg

m

The area of a rectangle

MEASURES, SHAPE AND SPACE

Achieved?

Hurray! There is an easy way to remember how to answer questions about the area of rectangles. Just remember this formula:

Area of a rectangle = the length × the width.

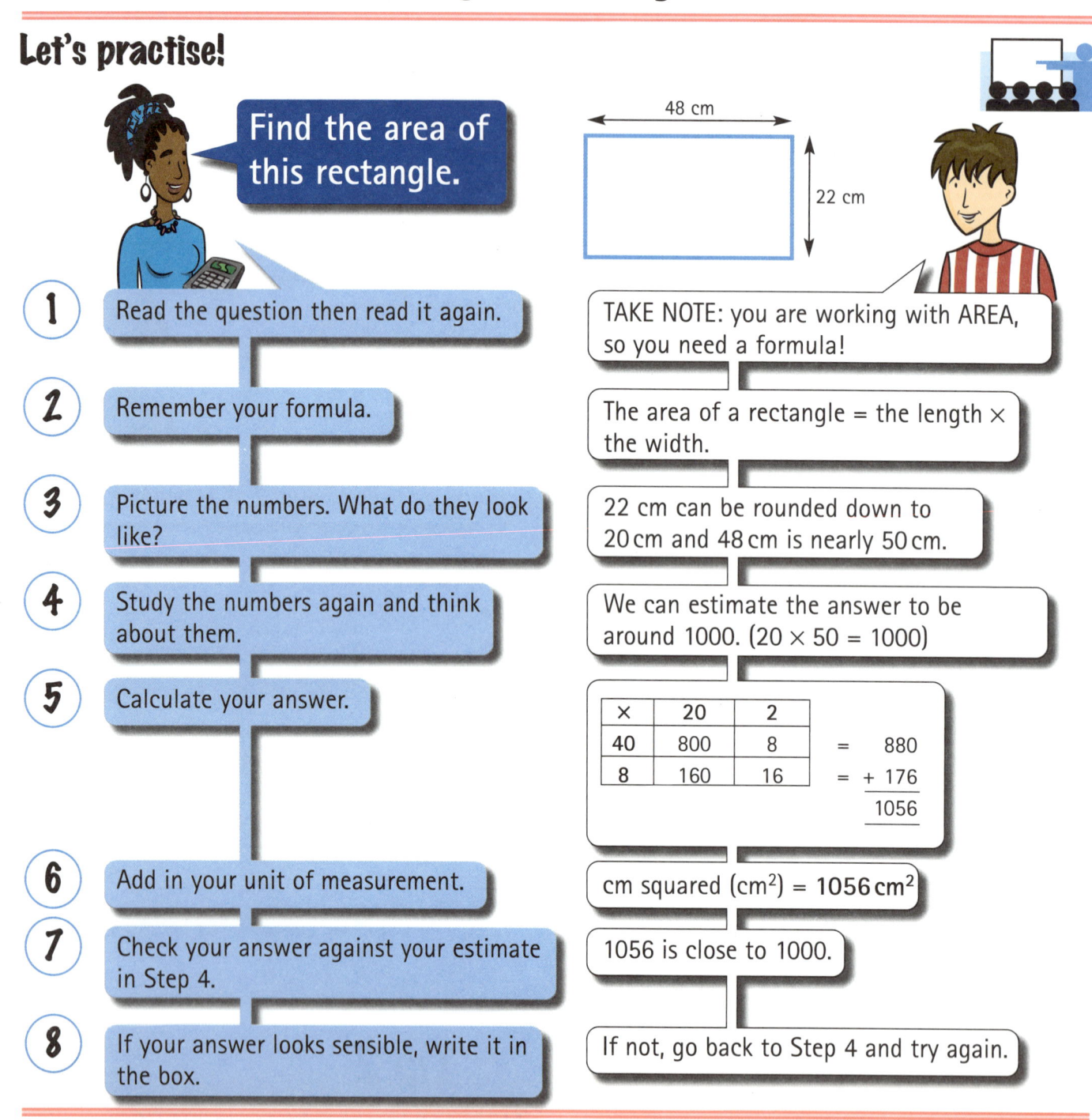

Let's practise!

Find the area of this rectangle.

48 cm
22 cm

1. Read the question then read it again. — TAKE NOTE: you are working with AREA, so you need a formula!

2. Remember your formula. — The area of a rectangle = the length × the width.

3. Picture the numbers. What do they look like? — 22 cm can be rounded down to 20 cm and 48 cm is nearly 50 cm.

4. Study the numbers again and think about them. — We can estimate the answer to be around 1000. (20 × 50 = 1000)

5. Calculate your answer. —

×	20	2
40	800	8
8	160	16

= 880
= + 176
‾‾‾‾‾
1056

6. Add in your unit of measurement. — cm squared (cm²) = 1056 cm²

7. Check your answer against your estimate in Step 4. — 1056 is close to 1000.

8. If your answer looks sensible, write it in the box. — If not, go back to Step 4 and try again.

★ Tip 1

When dealing with area, make sure the units are ALWAYS squared.

e.g.   cm²   m²   km²

★ Tip 2

Break up complicated shapes into smaller rectangles to make the question easier to answer. Remember to add up the areas of all the rectangles to get your answer!

MEASURES, SHAPE AND SPACE 45

Let's try another question. Here is a shape you will have to divide up into smaller shapes.

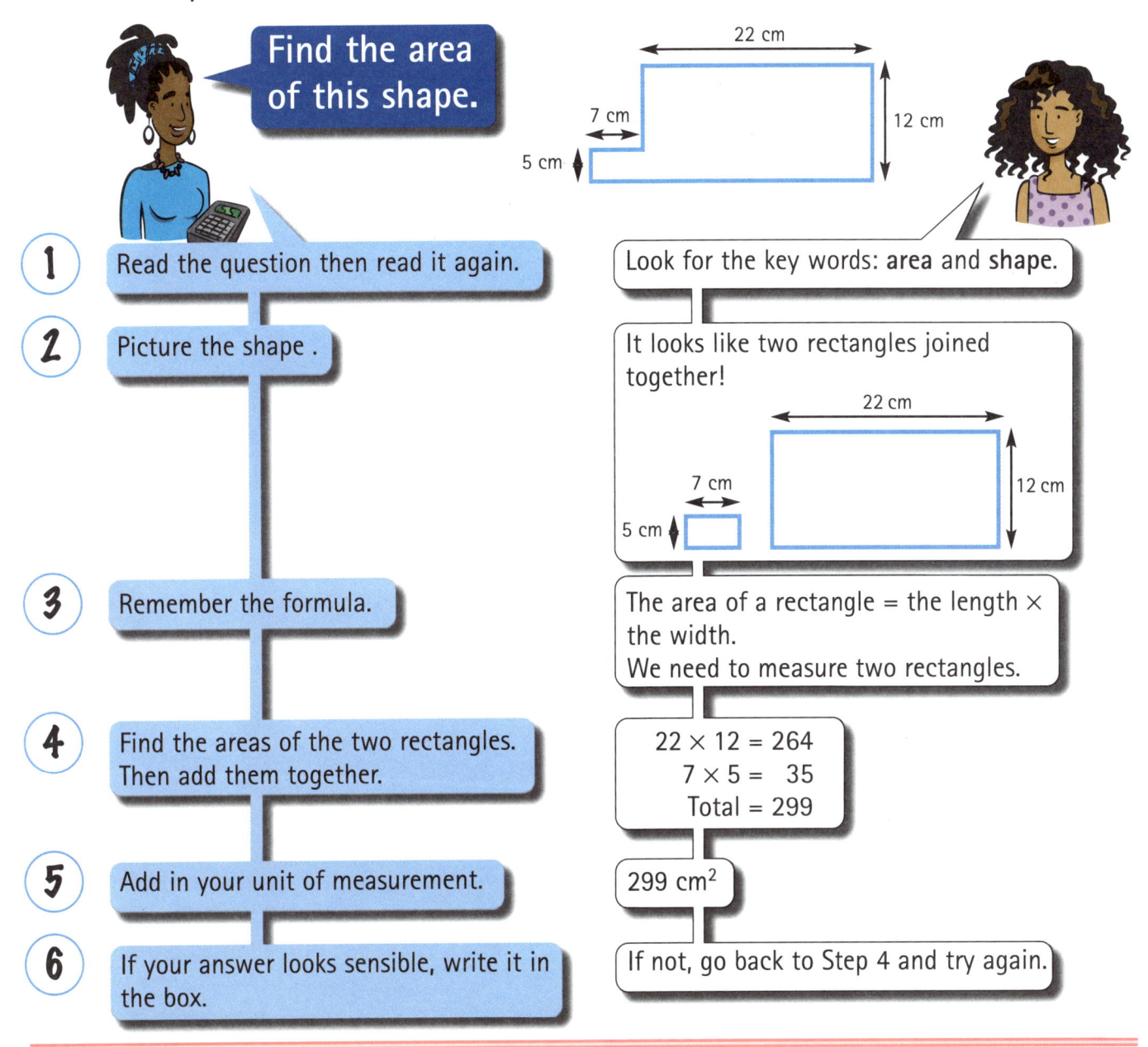

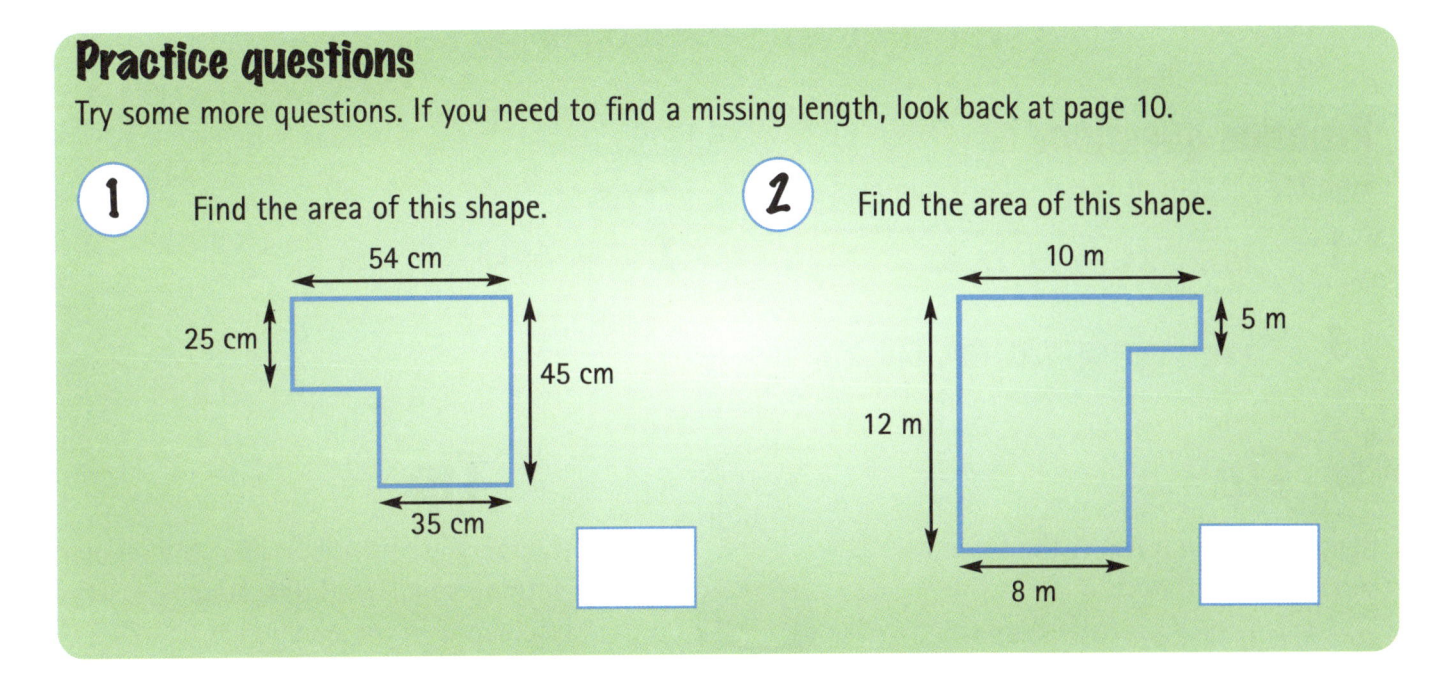

Find the area of this shape.

(1) Read the question then read it again. — Look for the key words: **area** and **shape**.

(2) Picture the shape. — It looks like two rectangles joined together!

(3) Remember the formula. — The area of a rectangle = the length × the width. We need to measure two rectangles.

(4) Find the areas of the two rectangles. Then add them together.
22 × 12 = 264
7 × 5 = 35
Total = 299

(5) Add in your unit of measurement. — 299 cm²

(6) If your answer looks sensible, write it in the box. — If not, go back to Step 4 and try again.

Practice questions

Try some more questions. If you need to find a missing length, look back at page 10.

(1) Find the area of this shape.
54 cm, 25 cm, 45 cm, 35 cm

(2) Find the area of this shape.
10 m, 5 m, 12 m, 8 m

Finding the mean and median

Achieved?

The mean is the **average** of a group of numbers. To find the mean all you have to do is add all the amounts and divide the answer by the number of amounts. For example:

2, 2, 4, 6, 10, 12.
The mean = (2 + 2 + 4 + 6 + 10 + 12) ÷ 6
36 ÷ 6 = 6

The median is the **middle number** in a group of numbers. To find the median, put the numbers in order from smallest to largest and find the middle number. For example:

48, 23, 67, 94, 12, 73, 88
median = 12, 23, 48, 67, 73, 88, 94
= 67 (the middle number)

Practice questions
Find the mean of these sets of numbers.

1. 358, 321, 374, 311, 437, 223, 335
2. 5587, 4424, 5734, 5871, 6319
3. 7834, 5796, 4348, 5684, 7713

Practice questions
Find the median of these sets of numbers.

1. 19, 21, 23, 24, 23, 22, 22
2. 30, 55, 58, 51, 55, 48, 51, 52, 50
3. 121, 189, 184, 230, 164, 148, 215, 236, 169

★ **Tip**
Remember: the mean is the same as 'average'.

★ **Tip**
To help you remember what the median is, think *small*, *medium*, *large*. (Median is in the middle!)

Finding the range and mode

Achieved?

The range is the **difference** between the greatest and the least in a set of data. Here are the scores out of 100 for the contestants in the school quiz.

Let's practise!

53, 75, 25, 46, 89, 63, 37, 96

The range is 71 because 96 (the highest score) − 25 (the lowest score) = 71

Practice question
Find the ranges of these computer game scores.

1) 683, 449, 782, 790, 548, 224, 335 ☐

2) 592, 981, 581, 769, 327, 269, 832 ☐

3) 990, 358, 572, 894, 336, 592, 779 ☐

The mode is the **most common** value in a group of numbers. To find the mode, sort the numbers into sets of the same amount. Look for the set with the most numbers. For example: 23, 24, 25, 21, 24, 23, 24, 25, 23, 23

Group the numbers
21
23, 23, 23, 23
24, 24, 24
25, 25
23 is the mode of this set.

Practice question
Find the mode of these computer game scores out of a thousand.

1) 550, 554, 556, 554, 557, 556, 554, 557, 556, 554 ☐

2) 332, 336, 354, 336, 355, 336, 334, 355, 336, 334 ☐

3) 423, 425, 463, 442, 423, 423, 422, 442, 422, 423, 423 ☐

★ **Tip**
When finding the range, write the numbers in order of size.

★ **Tip**
Mode is the *most common* value.

Graphs and pie charts

Achieved?

To get a Level 5 you will need to look at graphs like the one below and answer questions about them.

Let's practise!

These road signs are in miles. Use the conversion graph to rewrite the road signs in kilometres.

Exeter 40 miles → Exeter ☐ km
Torquay 25 miles → Torquay ☐ km
Newton Abbot 15 miles → Newton Abbot ☐ km

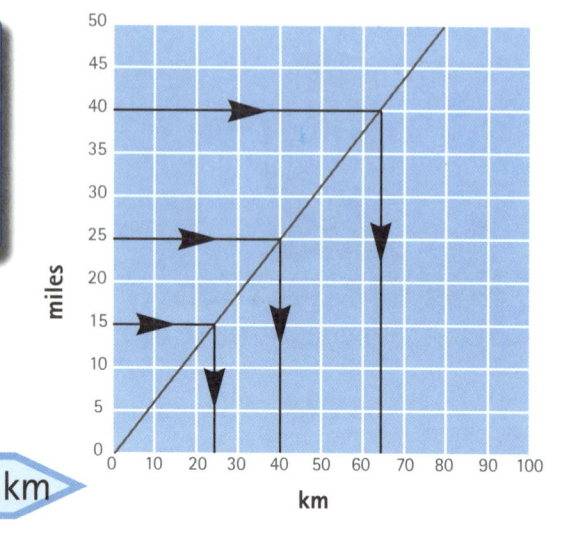

1 Read the question then read it again.

Conversion graph tells us that we need to convert values.

2 Be methodical.

Exeter
- We need to change 40 miles into kilometres.
- Go up the y axis (miles) and find 40.
- Mark this point on the y axis with your pencil.
- Go across to the conversion line and make another mark.
- Now go down to find out the value in kilometres.

Our answer is nearly halfway between 60 and 70, so we can estimate 64 km! Now repeat for Torquay and Newton Abbot.

3 Does the answer look sensible? If so, fill in the answer box.

Check your answers carefully on the graph before writing them in the boxes. The test marker is looking for an EXACT answer.

Practice question

The exchange rate for pounds to euros is £1 = €1.6. Using the graph above to help you, draw a new graph to convert pounds to euros. Use the graph to find out how much you would receive when you exchange:

(a) £55 = € ☐   (b) £40 = € ☐

(c) €35 = £ ☐   (d) €72 = £ ☐

HANDLING DATA 49

Pie charts are a way of showing ideas as a fraction, percentage or proportion. They are an excellent way of showing information quickly and clearly... as long as you know what to look for! Get used to seeing what the slices 'look like' so you can instantly recognise the proportions of a whole. It is worth drawing circles and practising dividing them into equal $\frac{1}{3}$, $\frac{1}{2}$, $\frac{1}{5}$, etc.

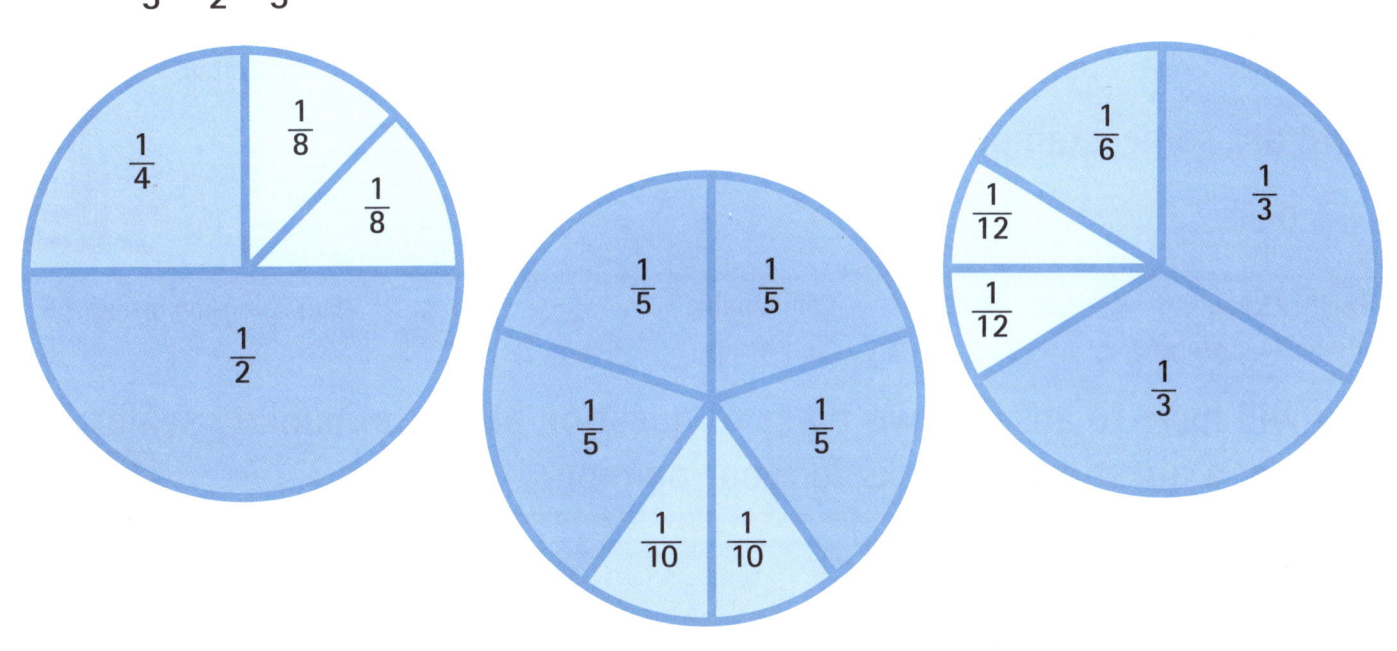

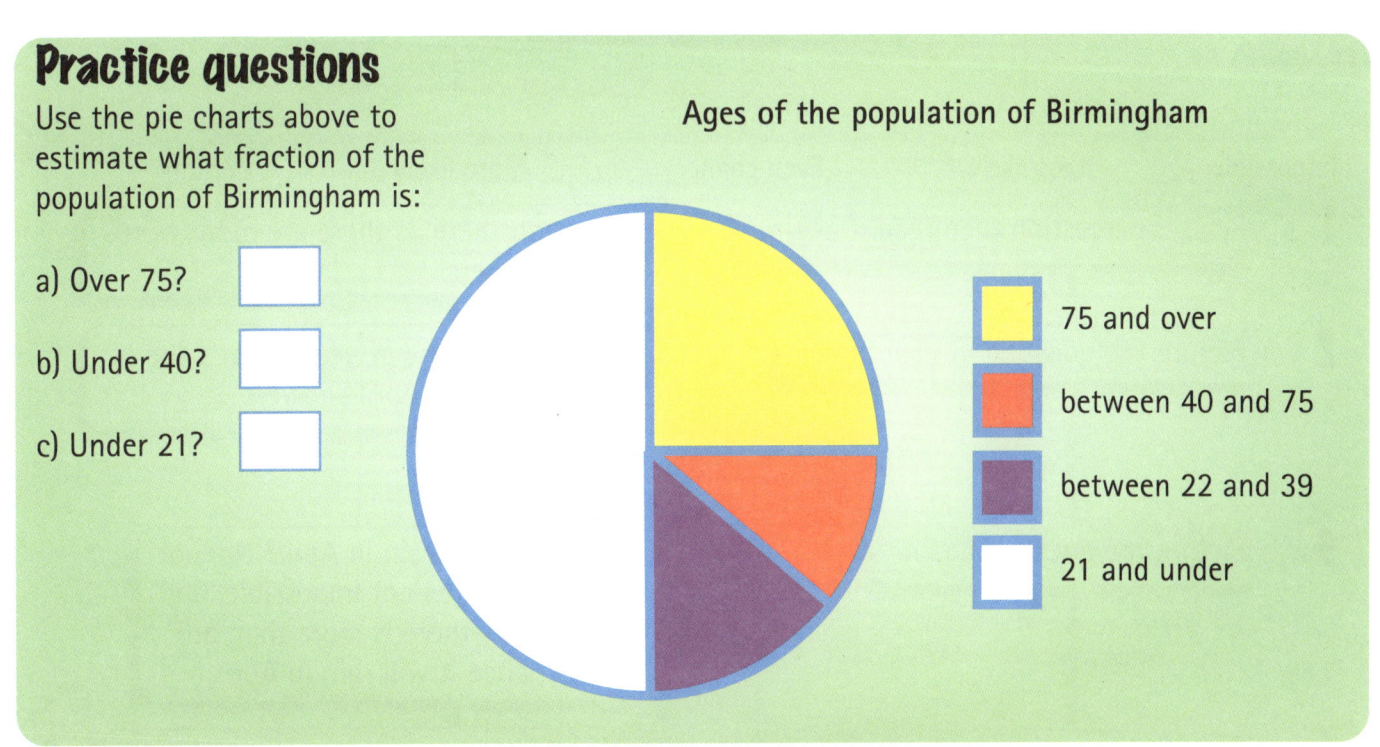

Practice questions

Use the pie charts above to estimate what fraction of the population of Birmingham is:

a) Over 75? ☐

b) Under 40? ☐

c) Under 21? ☐

Ages of the population of Birmingham

- 75 and over
- between 40 and 75
- between 22 and 39
- 21 and under

★ Tip 1

Be VERY careful when reading scales or axes. You may be asked to find values BETWEEN lines on the scale. A test marker would want to know if you can find the EXACT answer.

★ Tip 2

Always draw graphs and read graphs carefully and accurately.
A sharp pencil, straight ruler and steady hand are essential!

The probability scale

Achieved? 😊 😐 ☹️

The probability scale is a way of showing how likely something is to happen on a scale of 0 to 1.

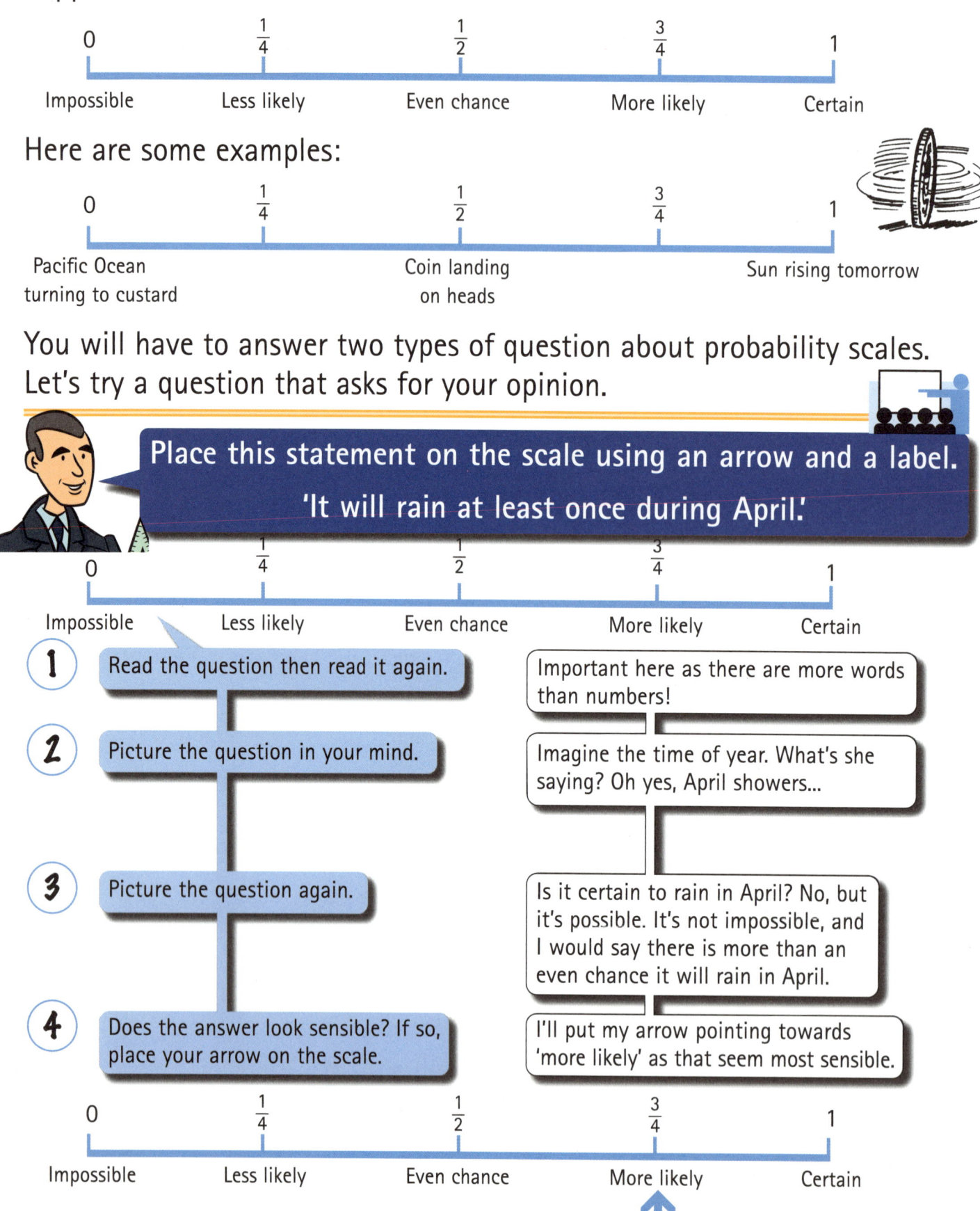

```
0        1/4        1/2        3/4        1
|---------|----------|----------|---------|
Impossible  Less likely  Even chance  More likely  Certain
```

Here are some examples:

```
0        1/4        1/2        3/4        1
|---------|----------|----------|---------|
Pacific Ocean          Coin landing        Sun rising tomorrow
turning to custard     on heads
```

You will have to answer two types of question about probability scales. Let's try a question that asks for your opinion.

> Place this statement on the scale using an arrow and a label.
> 'It will rain at least once during April.'

```
0        1/4        1/2        3/4        1
|---------|----------|----------|---------|
Impossible  Less likely  Even chance  More likely  Certain
```

1 Read the question then read it again. — Important here as there are more words than numbers!

2 Picture the question in your mind. — Imagine the time of year. What's she saying? Oh yes, April showers...

3 Picture the question again. — Is it certain to rain in April? No, but it's possible. It's not impossible, and I would say there is more than an even chance it will rain in April.

4 Does the answer look sensible? If so, place your arrow on the scale. — I'll put my arrow pointing towards 'more likely' as that seem most sensible.

```
0        1/4        1/2        3/4        1
|---------|----------|----------|---------|
Impossible  Less likely  Even chance  More likely  Certain
                                         ⬆
                              'It will rain at least once during April'
```

HANDLING DATA 51

Now let's try a probability question that asks for a mathematically correct answer.

These coloured balls were placed in a bag:

5 pink   30 blue   2 green   3 brown

Estimate the chance that the first ball to be taken out of the bag will be a blue ball and mark it on the probability scale.

① Read the question then read it again.

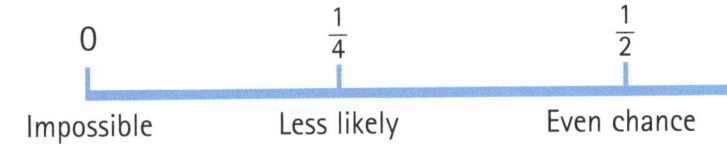

Words and numbers to think about. What is the question asking you to do?

② Picture the question in your mind.

Try to picture the different coloured balls going into the bag.

③ Add up the total number of balls.

5 + 30 + 2 + 3 = 40

④ How many of them are orange?

There are 30 blue balls.
So there are 30 blue balls out of 40.

⑤ Express your probability as a fraction, decimal or percentage. This is important!

This can be expressed as a fraction, percentage or decimal:

$\frac{3}{4}$ 75%   0.75

⑥ Decide where to place your arrow.

Draw the arrow three quarters of the way along the line. Be accurate here because the probability scale is clearly marked.

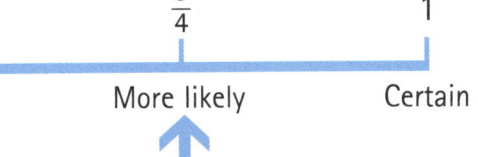

```
0         1/4         1/2         3/4         1
|----------|-----------|-----------|----------|
Impossible  Less likely  Even chance  More likely  Certain
                                      ↑
                              First ball will be blue
```

Practice question

There are 32 doughnuts in a bag. 14 are jam, 2 are chocolate and the rest are apple.
What are the chances of taking an appple doughnut out of the bag?
(a) Write your answer down as a fraction, decimal or percentage.
(b) Draw your answer on this probability scale.

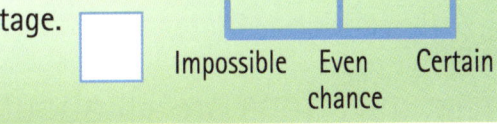

Impossible   Even chance   Certain

★ Tip 1

When throwing a dice there is an EQUAL chance of rolling any of the numbers.
When tossing a coin there is an EQUAL chance of getting heads or tails.

★ Tip 2

If you are not marking a probability on a scale, you must present it as a **fraction**, **decimal** or **percentage**.

Using and applying mathematics

Achieved? 😊 😐 ☹

Introduction

The reason for learning all the different mathematical skills (multiplying, dividing, measuring, estimating and so on) is so you can use them to solve mathematical problems.

Imagine learning all the shots in tennis, like the serve, the volley, the backhand and forehand, but never actually getting to play a game! Only by using your shots in a match will you learn to be a tennis player. Likewise, only by using your mathematical skills will you learn to be a mathematician!

The flow chart opposite is designed to guide you when tackling a maths problem. It will help organise your thinking, but it won't tell you the answer – that's for you to work out for yourself.

The next few pages contain problems for you to solve. Work through the examples first and then have a go at the practice questions using the flow chart approach.

Good luck!

Problem solving

NUMBER
These questions are all about your number skills. You must use them in the right way though!

MEASURES
These questions are all about real situations: going on a journey, the amount of milk a family drinks in a week and so on.

SHAPE AND SPACE
These questions all require you to use your knowledge about shapes, both 2D and 3D.

HANDLING DATA
These questions often ask you to find out information from a table or chart. They will also ask you to explain how you found out the answer!

USING AND APPLYING MATHEMATICS   53

The Problem Solving Flow Chart

1 Read the question then read it again. — Read through the question slowly. Twice. Let the words and numbers 'sink in'.

2 Picture the words and numbers. What do they mean? — What does this problem mean to you? You could draw a picture or diagram to help you. You could write it in your own words.

3 Highlight key words and phrases. — Look for mathematical phrases like 'find the difference between', and 'what is the product of'. Work out what is important information and what isn't.

4 Can you estimate an answer? — This will depend on the question. Estimate using the information you have. Don't guess wildly.

5 What calculations do you need to do? — Work out what needs to be added, subtracted, multiplied and divided. Sometimes you may need to perform more than one function. Write the calculations down but don't do them yet.

6 What is the answer to your calculations? Show how you got your answer. — Now calculate if you need to. Estimate first. Write down your method – it shows how well you are thinking. Check your answer.

7 What is the answer to the original problem? Write it in full sentences. — Does your answer match what you have been asked to do? Don't just give one word or number answers (e.g. 12). Write it in a clear sentence (e.g. The number that Sofie was thinking of was 12.)

8 Is your answer a sensible one? — Does your answer make sense? Is it realistic? If the problem is a real-life problem, have you got a real-life answer?

★ Tips

- ★ Remember your 'checking the answer' skills.
- ★ Think clearly and write clearly.
- ★ Present your work so it shows what you have done.
- ★ Work step-by-step.
- ★ Make a problem easier (e.g. Find 24 lots of 6. Try finding 4 lots first then 20 lots.)
- ★ Take a reasonable guess at what you think might happen.
- ★ Think HOW you are working. Change your method if something isn't working.
- ★ Look for patterns in your maths.

USING AND APPLYING MATHEMATICS

Solving number problems

Achieved?

Let's try a simple number problem.

The numbers in row 2 of this triangle of pool balls have been found from the two numbers directly above them using a rule. Fill in the missing numbers and write the rule.

Row 1 84 72 88 44
Row 2   78 80 66
Row 3
Row 4

Rule:

1 Read the question then read it again.

There are two things to do to complete this question – "find the missing numbers" and "write the rule".

2 Picture the words and numbers. What do they mean?

How are these numbers 'linked'? When we have worked it out, we need to *explain* how.

3 Highlight key words and phrases.

"numbers in row 2", "found from the two numbers directly above".

4 Can you estimate an answer?

No, because the answer is not immediately obvious.

5 What calculations do you need to do?

Work step-by-step. Start with 84 and 72. What do we have to do to get 78?
84 + 72 = or 84 – 72 =

6 What is the answer to your calculations? Show how you got your answer.

84 + 72 = 156 and 84 - 72 = 12. Look at our answers. Can we see any 'link' with 78? Yes! 156 is double 78 or 78 is half 156. We have found the rule!

7 What is the answer to the original problem? Write it in full sentences.

The rule is add the two numbers together and divide the total by two. We can also fill in the missing numbers.
(78 + 80) ÷ 2 = 79 and (80 + 66) ÷ 2 = 73
so (79 + 73) ÷ 2 = 76

8 Is your answer a sensible one?

Yes, we can test our rule throughout the triangle. It works!

USING AND APPLYING MATHEMATICS 55

Practice questions

Use the flow chart to help you to answer these number problem questions.

1

Mary's Fashions
Sequin Disco top £8.99
Mr Seventy Jeans £3.49
Sadie's Sunglasses

Mylee paid for her clothes with a £50 note.
She got £2.89 change.
How much were her sunglasses?
Show your method.

Answer:

2

Pets R Us
3 x mice @ £8.99 each
2 x parrots @ £13.25 each
1 x hamster @ £3.99 each
25% discount
Total

Nick and Stephen are starting a petting zoo. They bought 3 mice for £8.99 each, 2 parrots for £13.25 each and a hamster for £3.99 from Pets R Us. They used their discount card and got 25% off. How much did they pay in total? Show your method. Remember to round your answer to the nearest penny.

Answer:

3 Put the numbers 1 to 9 into this grid so that the columns and the diagonals each equal 15. Investigate other magic squares.

4 I think of a number, I multiply it by 9 and subtract 45.

My answer is 36. What was my number? Show your method.

What do you notice about all of the numbers?

Solving measures problems

Achieved?

Let's try this simple measures problem.

> Here is a list of ingredients for Jimmie's jam tarts.
> It makes 12 jam tarts.
> 180 g plain flour   6 teaspoons of water
> 80 g of butter   120 g of strawberry jam
> 12 fresh strawberries
> Jimmy is having some extra friends round for tea and wants to make 15 of his special tarts. Can you change the amount of each ingredient so he cooks enough tarts?

1 Read the question then read it again. — Change the amounts of 5 ingredients…

2 Picture the words and numbers. What do they mean? — We could draw each item.

3 Highlight key words and phrases. — Change the amounts so there are enough tarts for 15 instead of 12… That's an increase of 25%!

4 Can you estimate an answer? — Not easy as there are lots of ingredients, but we know we are adding a 'quarter as much again' to each ingredient.

5 What calculations do you need to do? — 25% of 180 g, 80 g, 6 teaspoons, 120 g, 12 strawberries.

6 What is the answer to your calculations. Show how you got your answer. — 25% of 180 g = 45 g; 25% of 80 g = 20 g
25% of 6 teaspoons = 1.5 teaspoons;
25% of 120 g = 30 g
25% of 12 strawberries = 3 strawberries

7 What is the answer to the original problem? Write it in full sentences. — Jimmy would need 225 g of plain flour, 100 g of butter, 7.5 teaspoons of water, 150 g of jam and 15 strawberries.

8 Is your answer a sensible one? — Yes, we have increased the ingredients by the correct amounts.

56 USING AND APPLYING MATHEMATICS

USING AND APPLYING MATHEMATICS   57

Practice questions

Use the flow chart to help you to answer these questions about measures.

The Great Pyramid at Giza in Egypt is one of the Seven Ancient Wonders of the World and was the tallest building in the world for over 6000 years. Here are some facts about the Great Pyramid.

- The length of each side at it's base is 230.4 m
- It is 138 m tall and has four sides
- It was constructed from 2 300 000 limestone blocks
- Each block weighs on average, 2.5 tonnes
- The stones were cut from a quarry in Aswan; 800 km away.
- The estimated volume of the Great Pyramid is 2 500 000 cubic metres (1 cubic metre = 1000 litres)

1 If you ran twice around the base of the Great Pyramid, what would be the total distance you ran?

2 What would be the estimated weight of the Great Pyramid?

3 If a toy building block is 4 cm tall, how many would you need to build a tower as high as the Great Pyramid?

4 A ship carrying 150 limestone blocks on each trip made 7 return journeys from Aswan to the site of the Great Pyramid.
(a) How far did the ship travel?
(b) How many limestone blocks did it deliver?

5 If the Great Pyramid was hollow and you made a hole in the top, how many litres of water could you pour in?

58 USING AND APPLYING MATHEMATICS

Solving shape and space problems

Achieved?

Let's try a tricky shape and space problem.

> How many equilateral triangles can you see in this diagram? 
>
> Show your method:

1. Read the question then read it again.

   Study the words and the shape. Think past the obvious.

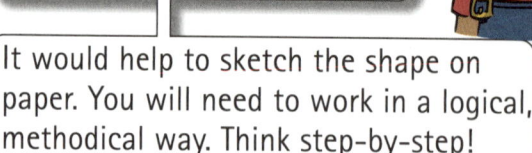

2. Picture the words and numbers. What do they mean?

   It would help to sketch the shape on paper. You will need to work in a logical, methodical way. Think step-by-step!

3. Highlight key words and phrases.

   How many. We are going to need the exact number of triangles to be correct. Miss one and we're wrong!

4. Can you estimate an answer?

   We can see 17 in front of us (16 little ones and the big one). 5 hidden, 22 in total.

5. What calculations do you need to do?

   Work in a logical way using a table. How many 1 triangles are there? How many 4 triangles are there? And so on...

6. What is the answer to your calculations? Show how you got your answer.

Number of smaller triangles in the big triangle	1	4	9	16	Total
Quantity seen	16	7	3	1	Total

7. What is the answer to the original problem? Write it in full sentences.

   We can see 27 equilateral triangles in the diagram.

8. Is your answer a sensible one?

   It looks sensible because we worked in a step-by-step way. Our estimate was quite close and a logical approach has given us the correct answer.

USING AND APPLYING MATHEMATICS 59

Practice questions

Use the flow chart to help you to answer these questions about shape and space.

1 How many rectangles are there within this shape?

2 This cube is made up of 8 smaller cubes. All the cubes are red. If the outside of the cube is painted blue and then taken apart, how many sides are red and how many are blue? You may like to record your answer in a table?

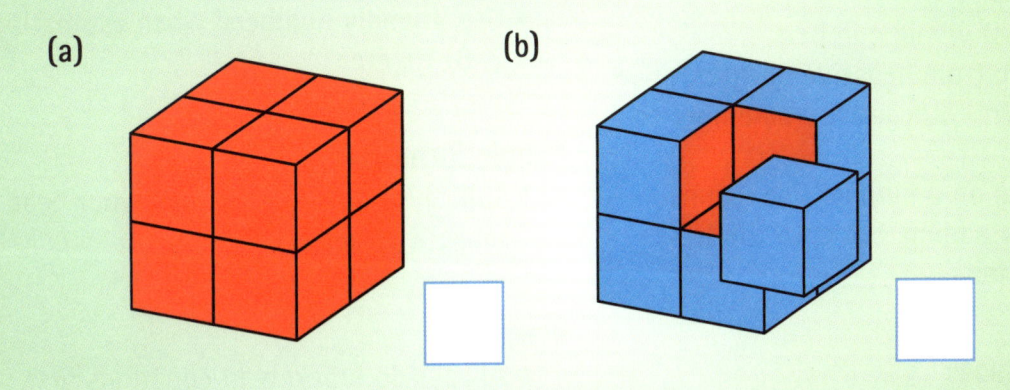

(a)

(b)

3 Trace over the tangram on plain paper and cut the pieces out. Make the shapes into a square. Investigate other 2D shapes you can make using the tangram pieces. Record your findings in a table.

KEY FACTS

The Number System and Calculations

Multiplying decimals by 10, 100 and 1000
- Shuffle numbers to the left.
- Shuffle numbers to the left once when × 10, twice when × 100 and three times when × 1000.

Dividing decimals by 10, 100 and 1000
- Shuffle numbers to the right.
- Shuffle numbers to the right once when ÷ by 10, twice when ÷ by 100, and three times when ÷ by 1000.

Negative numbers
- Integers are just whole numbers.
- When counting from negative up to positive or positive down to negative, remember to count 0!
- When counting on a number line, count to the right when adding, count to the left when subtracting.

Decimals to two places
- When rounding, remember 5 is up! 6.785 = 6.79

Reducing a fraction to its simplest form
- To reduce a fraction to its simplest form, find a common factor which you can divide into the numerator and the denominator. For example, $\frac{3}{9} \div \frac{3}{3} = \frac{1}{3}$

Calculating a fraction or percentage
- Remember as many percentage/fraction equivalents as you can:

  $50\% = \frac{1}{2}$ $25\% = \frac{1}{4}$ $75\% = \frac{3}{4}$

  $33\% =$ nearly $\frac{1}{3}$ $66\% =$ nearly $\frac{2}{3}$

Multiplication and division (with decimal points)
- × and ÷ are opposites.
- Always estimate first. It will help you to get the decimal point in the right place if one is needed.

Checking your answers
- Inverse means opposite!
- Check addition by subtraction – and vice versa.
- Check division by multiplication – and vice versa.
- Use 'friendly numbers' when estimating: 2, 5, 10, etc.

Simple formulae
- Talk through the formula in your head. It will make it easier.

Brackets
- Always do brackets in equations first.

Coordinates
- Always read ALONG (x axis) and then UP (y axis).
- Always write (x) before (y) – (x, y).
- Quadrants work **anti-clockwise**.

3 o'clock to 12 o'clock   = Quadrant 1
12 o'clock to 9 o'clock   = Quadrant 2
9 o'clock to 6 o'clock   = Quadrant 3
6 o'clock to 3 o'clock   = Quadrant 4

Measures, Shape and Space

2D shapes
- **Pentagon**
  Pentagons have FIVE sides.
  Regular pentagons have FIVE EQUAL SIDES.
- **Parallelogram**
  A parallelogram is a RECTANGLE THAT HAS BEEN PUSHED OVER.
  Remember the opposite sides are the same length but parallel.
- **Isosceles and scalene triangles**
  An isosceles triangle has TWO EQUAL SIDES AND TWO EQUAL ANGLES.
  Picture an isosceles triangle as an arrow!
  A scalene triangle has THREE SIDES OF DIFFERENT LENGTHS and THREE ANGLES OF DIFFERENT sizes.
  When picturing a scalene triangle, think of SCALING A MOUNTAIN that has an easy way up or a more difficult side to climb!

Angles
- Acute angle = 0–89°
- Right angle = 90°
- Obtuse angle = 91–179°
- Straight line = 180°
- Reflex angle = 181–359°
- Angles around a POINT always add up to 360° (a complete turn).
- The angles of a TRIANGLE always add up to 180°.

Symmetries
- When drawing reflections, remember to keep the correct distance from the mirror line.

Metric and imperial conversions (approximate)
- 1 litre = 1.8 pints
- 1 kilogram = 2.2 lbs (pounds)
- 1 pound = 0.454 kg
- 1 mile = 1.6 km
- 5 miles = 8 km
- 1 foot = 30 cm
- 1 metre = 3 feet 3 inches
- 1 inch = 2.5 cm

Estimating measures
- Milli = very small
- Centi = small
- Kilo = big

Area of a rectangle
- Area of a rectangle = length (L) × width (W)
- Area is always units squared (cm^2, m^2, mm^2)

Handling Data

Pictograms
- With pictograms PICTURE = NUMBER
  e.g. ♀ = 20 ice creams   ſ = 10 ice creams

Mean, median, range, mode
- Mean = sum of all numbers divided by number of numbers
- Median = middle number in sequence (always write down in order first)
- Range = difference between highest and lowest number
- Mode = most common value

Charts and graphs
- Be careful and accurate. Use a sharp pencil.
- Pie charts are good for percentages, fractions or decimals.

Probability scale
- Always goes from 0 to 1 (you need fractions/decimals here).

0	0.25	0.5	0.75	1
Impossible	Less likely	Even chance	More likely	Certain

Tips and technique

Before a test

1. When you revise, try revising a 'little and often' rather than in long sessions.
2. Learn your multiplication facts up to 10 × 10 so that you can recall them instantly. These are your tools for performing your calculations.
3. Revise with a friend. You can encourage and learn from each other.
4. Get a good night's sleep the night before.
5. Be prepared – bring your own pens and pencils and wear a watch to check the time as you go.

During a test

1. Don't rush the first few questions. These tend to be quite straightforward, so don't make any silly mistakes.
2. As you know by now, READ THE QUESTION THEN READ IT AGAIN.
3. If you get stuck, don't linger on the same question – move on! You can come back to it later.
4. Never leave a multiple choice question. Make an educated guess if you really can't work out the answer.
5. Check to see how many marks a question is worth. Have you 'earned' those marks with your answer?
6. Check your answers. You can use the inverse method or the rounding method. Does your answer look correct?
7. Be aware of the time. After 20 minutes, check to see how far you have got.
8. Try to leave a couple of minutes at the end to read through what you have written.
9. Always show your method. You may get a mark for showing you have gone through the correct procedure even if your answer is wrong.
10. Don't leave any questions unanswered. In the two minutes you have left yourself at the end, make an educated guess at the questions you really couldn't do.

Answers

LEVEL 4 – TRICKY BITS

Page 8 – Predicting sequences
1) 53, 59   2) 148, 165, 199   3) –25, –36

Page 9 – Calculators
1) 1377   2) 599.4   3) 37.25   4) 326.8   5) 7796.89   6) 10 100

Page 11 – The 24 hour clock
1) 8hrs and 18 mins   2) 8hrs and 27 minutes   3) 2hrs and 49 minutes   4) 4hrs and 4 minutes

Page 12 – Reading scales
1) 160 ml   2) 90 ml

THE NUMBER SYSTEM AND CALCULATIONS

Page 14 – Checking your answers
1) $74 \times 45 = 3330$ ($3330 \div 45 = 74$)   2) $792 + 445 = 1237$ ($1237 - 445 = 792$)
3) $24624 \div 36 = 684$ ($684 \times 36 = 24624$)   4) $5823 - 771 = 5052$ ($5052 + 771 = 5823$)

Page 15 – Rounding up or down
1) $31 \times 59 = 1829$ ($30 \times 60 = 1800$)   2) $7992 - 295 = 7697$ ($8000 - 300 = 7700$)
3) $8192 + 209 = 8401$ ($8200 + 200 = 8400$)   4) $882 \div 18 = 49$ ($900 \div 20 = 45$)

Page 17 – Decimals
1) 23.75   2) 7.57   3) 42.53   4) £36.49

Page 18 – Reducing fractions
1) $\frac{5}{8}$ 2) $\frac{4}{9}$ 3) $\frac{7}{10}$ 4) $\frac{3}{8}$

Page 19 – Ratio and proportion
1) 1:3   2) $\frac{1}{4}$

Page 21 – Calculating fractions or percentages
1) 600 cm   2) 117 kg   3) £144   4) 33 km   5) 60 ml   6) £196
1) 38%   2) 15%   3) 35%   4) 65%

Page 23 – Multiplication and division
1) 17 352   2) 74 475   3) 31 726   4) 16 744   5) 11 880
6) 58   7) 27   8) 77   9) 55   10) 27

Page 25 – Negative numbers
1) –4, –1, 0, 2, 3   2) –25, –17, –11, –5, –3, 17   3) –7°   4) 5°

Page 27 – Simple formulae
1) T = £14   2) N = 20   3) P = £8   Formula M = (J × 7) + 7

Page 29 – Using brackets
1) 8610   2) 3532   3) 2769   4) 3718   5) 236   6) 73

Page 32 – Coordinates
1) (–1, 4) = 2nd Quadrant   (5, –3) = 4th Quadrant   (3, 1) = 1st Quadrant   (–2, –1) = 3rd Quadrant
2) (1, 0) (4, 0) (5, 2) (2, 2)

Page 33 – Angles
(a) 30°   (b) 115°   (c) 210°

ANSWERS

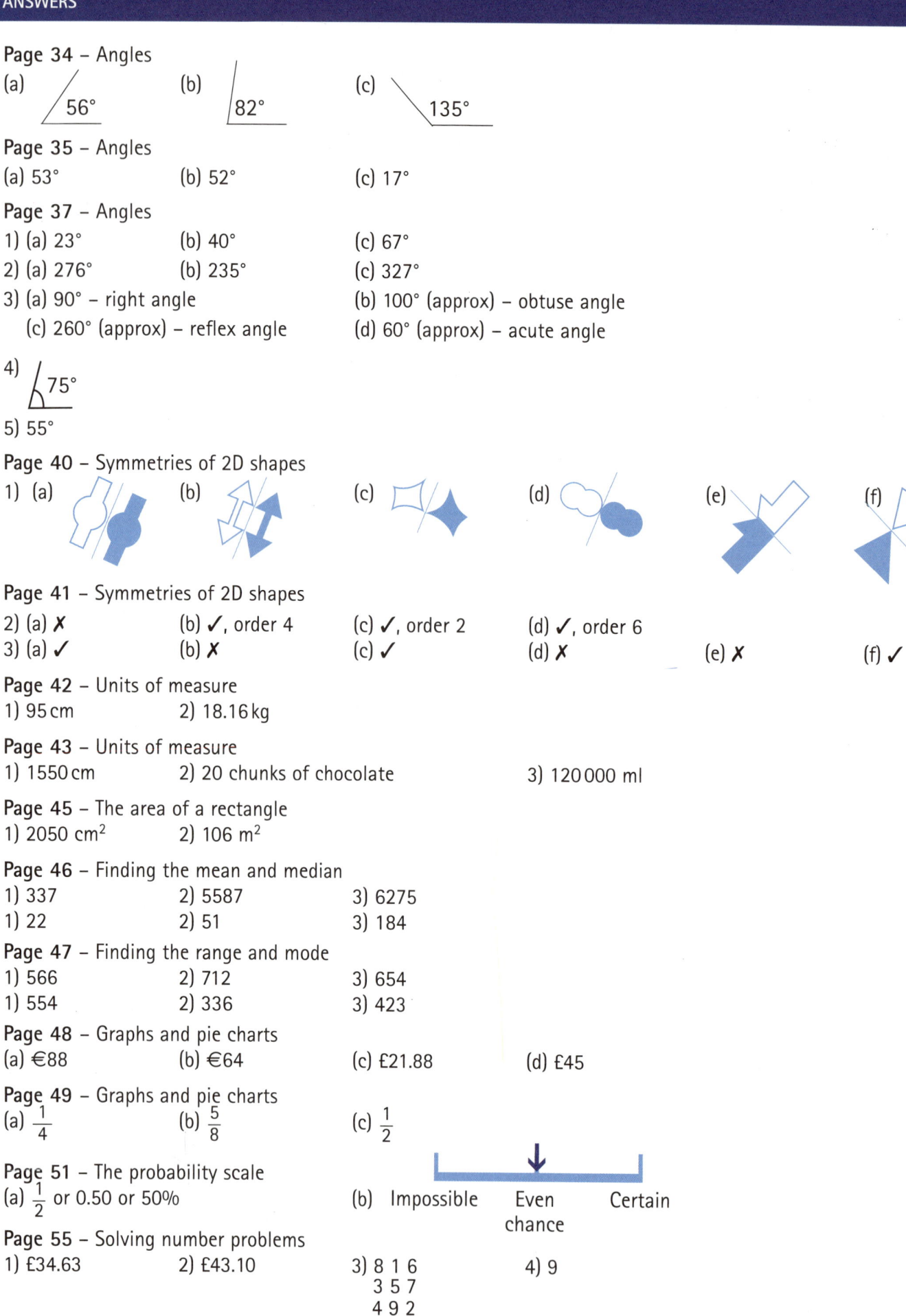

Page 34 – Angles
(a) 56°   (b) 82°   (c) 135°

Page 35 – Angles
(a) 53°   (b) 52°   (c) 17°

Page 37 – Angles
1) (a) 23°   (b) 40°   (c) 67°
2) (a) 276°   (b) 235°   (c) 327°
3) (a) 90° – right angle   (b) 100° (approx) – obtuse angle
   (c) 260° (approx) – reflex angle   (d) 60° (approx) – acute angle
4) 75°
5) 55°

Page 40 – Symmetries of 2D shapes
1) (a), (b), (c), (d), (e), (f)

Page 41 – Symmetries of 2D shapes
2) (a) ✗   (b) ✓, order 4   (c) ✓, order 2   (d) ✓, order 6
3) (a) ✓   (b) ✗   (c) ✓   (d) ✗   (e) ✗   (f) ✓

Page 42 – Units of measure
1) 95 cm   2) 18.16 kg

Page 43 – Units of measure
1) 1550 cm   2) 20 chunks of chocolate   3) 120 000 ml

Page 45 – The area of a rectangle
1) 2050 cm²   2) 106 m²

Page 46 – Finding the mean and median
1) 337   2) 5587   3) 6275
1) 22   2) 51   3) 184

Page 47 – Finding the range and mode
1) 566   2) 712   3) 654
1) 554   2) 336   3) 423

Page 48 – Graphs and pie charts
(a) €88   (b) €64   (c) £21.88   (d) £45

Page 49 – Graphs and pie charts
(a) $\frac{1}{4}$ (b) $\frac{5}{8}$ (c) $\frac{1}{2}$

Page 51 – The probability scale
(a) $\frac{1}{2}$ or 0.50 or 50%   (b) Impossible — Even chance — Certain

Page 55 – Solving number problems
1) £34.63   2) £43.10   3) 8 1 6 / 3 5 7 / 4 9 2   4) 9

Page 57 – Solving measures problems
1) 1843.2 m   2) 5 750 000 tonnes   3) 3450 toy blocks   4) (a) 11 200 km   (b) 1050 limestone blocks
5) 2 500 000 000 litres

Page 59 – Solving shape and space problems
1) 90   2) 24 sides are blue, 24 sides are red   3)